Henry Ford

These and other titles are included in The Importance Of biography series:

Maya Angelou	Martin Luther King Jr.
Louis Armstrong	Bruce Lee
James Baldwin	John Lennon
Lucille Ball	Abraham Lincoln
The Beatles	Charles Lindbergh
Alexander Graham Bell	Joe Louis
Napoléon Bonaparte	Douglas MacArthur
Julius Caesar	Thurgood Marshall
Rachel Carson	Margaret Mead
Charlie Chaplin	Golda Meir
Charlemagne	Mother Teresa
Winston Churchill	Muhammad
Christopher Columbus	John Muir
Leonardo da Vinci	Richard M. Nixon
James Dean	Pablo Picasso
Charles Dickens	Edgar Allan Poe
Walt Disney	Elvis Presley
F. Scott Fitzgerald	Queen Elizabeth I
Anne Frank	Queen Victoria
Benjamin Franklin	Eleanor Roosevelt
Mohandas Gandhi	Franklin D. Roosevelt
John Glenn	Jonas Salk
Jane Goodall	Margaret Sanger
Martha Graham	Oskar Schindler
Lorraine Hansberry	Dr. Seuss
Stephen Hawking	William Shakespeare
Ernest Hemingway	Frank Sinatra
Adolf Hitler	Tecumseh
Harry Houdini	Jim Thorpe
Thomas Jefferson	Pancho Villa
Mother Jones	Simon Wiesenthal
John F. Kennedy	The Wright Brothers

THE IMPORTANCE OF

Henry Ford

by Rafael Tilton

LUCENT BOOKS®

THOMSON

TM

GALE

San Diego • Detroit • New York • San Francisco • Cleveland • New Haven, Conn. • Waterville, Maine • London • Munich

On cover: Henry Ford sits in his first car, the quadricycle, in 1896.

© 2003 by Lucent Books. Lucent Books is an imprint of The Gale Group, Inc.,
a division of Thomson Learning, Inc.

Lucent Books® and Thomson Learning™ are trademarks used herein under license.

For more information, contact
Lucent Books
27500 Drake Rd.
Farmington Hills, MI 48331-3535
Or you can visit our Internet site at http://www.gale.com

LIBRARY OF CONGRESS CATALOGING-IN-PUBLICATION DATA

Tilton, Rafael.
    Henry Ford / by Rafael Tilton.
        p. cm. — (The Importance of)
    Includes bibliographical references and index.
    Summary: Discusses the early life of Henry Ford, including his moving to the big city
    and his success as an inventor, engineer, and pioneer of the automobile.
        ISBN 1-56006-846-9
        1. Ford, Henry, 1863–1947—Juvenile literature. 2. Industrialists—United States—
    Biography—Juvenile literature. 3. Automobile engineers—United States—Juvenile
    literature. [1. Ford, Henry, 1863–1947. 2. Industrialists. 3. Automobile industry and
    trade—Biography.] I. Title. II. Series.
        TL140.F6 T55 2002
        338.7'6292'092—dc21

    2003006212

Printed in the United States of America

Contents

Foreword

THE IMPORTANCE OF biography series deals with individuals who have made a unique contribution to history. The editors of the series have deliberately chosen to cast a wide net and include people from all fields of endeavor. Individuals from politics, music, art, literature, philosophy, science, sports, and religion are all represented. In addition, the editors did not restrict the series to individuals whose accomplishments have helped change the course of history. Of necessity, this criterion would have eliminated many whose contribution was great, though limited. Charles Darwin, for example, was responsible for radically altering the scientific view of the natural history of the world. His achievements continue to impact the study of science today. Others, such as Chief Joseph of the Nez Percé, played a pivotal role in the history of their own people. While Joseph's influence does not extend much beyond the Nez Percé, his nonviolent resistance to white expansion and his continuing role in protecting his tribe and his homeland remain an inspiration to all.

These biographies are more than factual chronicles. Each volume attempts to emphasize an individual's contributions both in his or her own time and for posterity. For example, the voyages of Christopher Columbus opened the way to European colonization of the New World. Unquestionably, his encounter with the New World brought monumental changes to both Europe and the Americas in his day. Today, however, the broader impact of Columbus's voyages is being critically scrutinized. *Christopher Columbus*, as well as every biography in The Importance Of series, includes and evaluates the most recent scholarship available on each subject.

Each author includes a wide variety of primary and secondary source quotations to document and substantiate his or her work. All quotes are footnoted to show readers exactly how and where biographers derive their information, as well as to provide stepping stones to further research. These quotations enliven the text by giving readers eyewitness views of the life and times of each individual covered in The Importance Of series.

Finally, each volume is enhanced by photographs, bibliographies, chronologies, and comprehensive indexes. For both the casual reader and the student engaged in research, The Importance Of biographies will be a fascinating adventure into the lives of people who have helped shape humanity's past and present, and who will continue to shape its future.

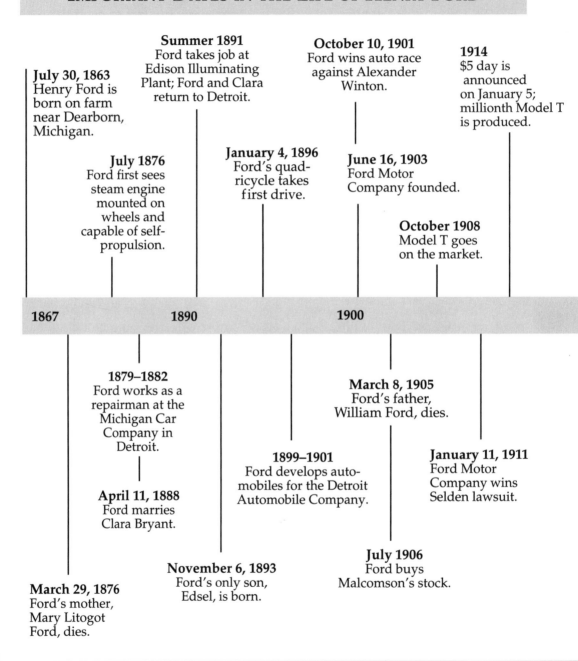

IMPORTANT DATES IN THE LIFE OF HENRY FORD

Summer 1891
Ford takes job at Edison Illuminating Plant; Ford and Clara return to Detroit.

October 10, 1901
Ford wins auto race against Alexander Winton.

1914
$5 day is announced on January 5; millionth Model T is produced.

July 30, 1863
Henry Ford is born on farm near Dearborn, Michigan.

July 1876
Ford first sees steam engine mounted on wheels and capable of self-propulsion.

January 4, 1896
Ford's quad-ricycle takes first drive.

June 16, 1903
Ford Motor Company founded.

October 1908
Model T goes on the market.

1867

1890

1900

1879–1882
Ford works as a repairman at the Michigan Car Company in Detroit.

March 8, 1905
Ford's father, William Ford, dies.

April 11, 1888
Ford marries Clara Bryant.

1899–1901
Ford develops auto-mobiles for the Detroit Automobile Company.

January 11, 1911
Ford Motor Company wins Selden lawsuit.

March 29, 1876
Ford's mother, Mary Litogot Ford, dies.

November 6, 1893
Ford's only son, Edsel, is born.

July 1906
Ford buys Malcomson's stock.

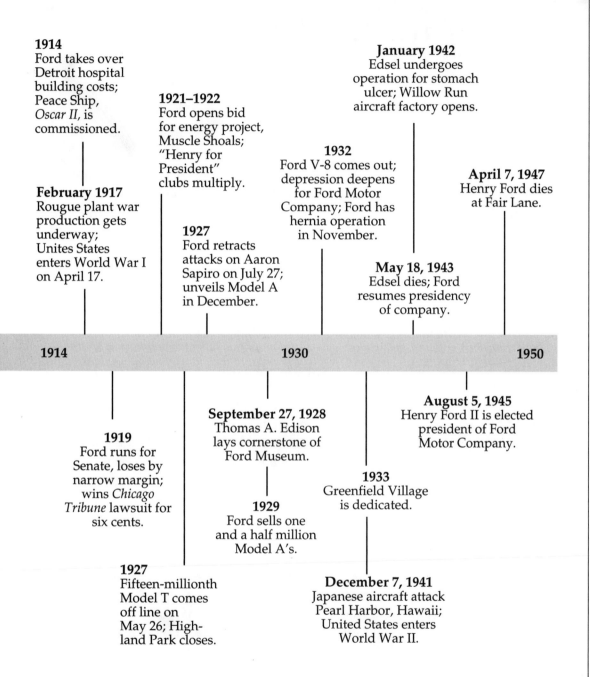

1914
Ford takes over Detroit hospital building costs; Peace Ship, *Oscar II,* is commissioned.

February 1917
Rouge plant war production gets underway; Unites States enters World War I on April 17.

1921–1922
Ford opens bid for energy project, Muscle Shoals; "Henry for President" clubs multiply.

1927
Ford retracts attacks on Aaron Sapiro on July 27; unveils Model A in December.

January 1942
Edsel undergoes operation for stomach ulcer; Willow Run aircraft factory opens.

1932
Ford V-8 comes out; depression deepens for Ford Motor Company; Ford has hernia operation in November.

April 7, 1947
Henry Ford dies at Fair Lane.

May 18, 1943
Edsel dies; Ford resumes presidency of company.

1914   **1930**   **1950**

1919
Ford runs for Senate, loses by narrow margin; wins *Chicago Tribune* lawsuit for six cents.

September 27, 1928
Thomas A. Edison lays cornerstone of Ford Museum.

1929
Ford sells one and a half million Model A's.

1933
Greenfield Village is dedicated.

August 5, 1945
Henry Ford II is elected president of Ford Motor Company.

1927
Fifteen-millionth Model T comes off line on May 26; High-land Park closes.

December 7, 1941
Japanese aircraft attack Pearl Harbor, Hawaii; United States enters World War II.

A Leader in the Field

Henry Ford I was the man who foresaw the United States becoming a nation of automobile drivers, and he devoted his life to making that goal a reality. Almost from the beginning, Ford measured his success in this area by the practicality of his product. Even while attending grade school in rural Michigan, he became interested in laborsaving design; as a boy, he developed a gate latch he could unfasten without getting off his wagon. Then in his teens, he went to Detroit to work as an engineer. He was repairing and running steam engines before he was twenty. And when, as a young adult, he first heard of an engine that burned gasoline to produce power, he knew he wanted to use such an engine to invent a machine that would make farmers' work easier.

Ford's development of that engine, a gasoline motor, occupied the first twenty years of his adult life. Completely engaged with what seemed like endless tinkering, he figured out a way to control the power of exploding gasoline. Soon, he used this discovery to power a motor that could turn the wheels of a wagon-like vehicle, what he called the "quadricycle." He went on to use what he learned from the quadricycle to produce a race car and a delivery truck.

Over time, he worked toward creating a vehicle that was strong, reliable, and economical. The result, the Model T Ford car, transported the United States into the twentieth century.

With an intense desire never to waste time, materials, or energy, Ford next began to devise economical methods of building his car. His assembly process changed rapidly over the first few years of Model T production. From an assembly process that used many hours of manpower, he progressed to a process that utilized moving belts and overhead pulleys to assist workers. This process, called the moving assembly line, sped up the construction of cars by eliminating unproductive movements. For instance, workers themselves no longer carried parts to and from workstations . Instead, belts, slides, and pulleys did that work.

Ford also implemented other practices that would increase profits for his company. Realizing that there were many lower-income buyers who would like to own cars, he lowered his prices and made a lot of money by selling to the multitude, rather than just to the rich. Seeing that the more cars he sold, the more profits he

Henry Ford was an inventor and a pioneer of American capitalism.

would make, he made his factories run faster and more efficiently. Realizing the importance of employees' working safely and rapidly, he spent money on training. Finally, he developed a sales force that brought his cars to more people than anyone thought possible.

These monumental achievements did not obscure some of Ford's more unfavorable traits, however. Ford's driving will sometimes led him to sacrifice his family, friends, and fellow workers, even his own ideal of honesty, in the pursuit of efficiency. Ford also had many strong ideas, including prejudices. And his seemingly endless energy and innate frugality led him to dis-like philanthropy, which he considered counterproductive.

Nevertheless, many of the positive effects of Ford's work remain today. His name is connected with two of the most visited institutions in the United States: the Henry Ford Museum and Greenfield Village. These continue to provide education and entertainment for thousands of visitors each year. There is also abundant affordable transportation today, not only in the United States but throughout most of the industrialized world. Finally, Ford's functioning principle, that good business is good for everybody, remains an ideal of the American capitalist economy.

1 Farm Mechanic

Henry Ford was born on a farm near Dearborn, Michigan, a few miles west of Detroit, on July 30, 1863. His father, William Ford, was an Irish immigrant who had followed his uncles and brothers to the United States during a famine in their home country. Once in America, William Ford first worked as a railroad carpenter, then bought land and turned to farming. One of his neighbors later said, "I knew Henry Ford's father like my own. He was a nice, quiet old man. He was a pretty good farmer . . . an easygoing old fellow. He was justice of the peace [and] . . . was pretty well liked by everyone."[1]

William Ford married Henry's mother, Mary Litogot, on April 25, 1861. At twenty-two, Mary was thirteen years younger than her new husband. Despite her youth, Mary Ford was a hard worker. She had grown up on a farm and readily accepted the duties that came with married life.

A Michigan Farm

Soon after their wedding, William and Mary Ford moved into a clapboard house on ninety acres of land. William Ford enjoyed his life as a farmer. He worked daily at the chores his large farm demanded.

Says biographer James Brough, "[William Ford] felled stands of virgin woodland with the help of ox teams and hauled the cut trees down the splintered plank road to the city on Saturdays for sale as fuel and lumber. He harvested wheat, oats, corn, hay and crops of apples and peaches, selling the surplus. He kept cows, pigs, sheep, and horses."[2]

The Fords' first child, a girl, lived only a few hours. She was followed by Henry and five others: John, born in 1865; Margaret, born in 1867; Jane, born in 1869; William Jr., born in 1871; and Robert, born in 1873.

Henry and his siblings spent their earliest days watching the farm activities of their parents—cooking, washing dishes, doing laundry, and tending to the animals and garden. As the oldest, Henry soon began to take part in these activities, and the older he got, the more responsibility he was asked to take on. He was put in charge of the horses, an important job on a farm where horses did all the heavy work. He also milked cows, plowed, and helped with the haying. The job he most enjoyed, however, was maintaining the tools in his father's blacksmith shop.

Yet it was not following in the footsteps of his farmer father that brought forth

Henry's deepest emotional response. According to Brough, "The parent Henry idolized was his overworked, bird-quick [brisk] mother—sewing, knitting, making soap, butter, and candles, tending to the chickens and the vegetable garden, looking after her increasing[ly] feeble . . . parents (who lived with the Fords), and teaching her eldest child to read before he entered school."[3]

SOUTH SETTLEMENT SCHOOL

When Henry turned seven, he began walking to South Settlement School, a red brick building a mile from his home. One teacher taught all the grades, and all the students crowded into a single room. Henry's sister Margaret describes the school's interior:

> The teacher's desk was on a platform raised one step so that she might see the students at the back of the room all the better. There were blackboards at the front of the room. As the teacher called the children to recite, they came to the front of the room. There was a piano on one side of the platform with the American flag close by. At the center front of the room was the wood stove. On winter mornings the teacher or a neighbor arrived early to start the fire and have the building warm when the children arrived at nine o'clock. The older boys

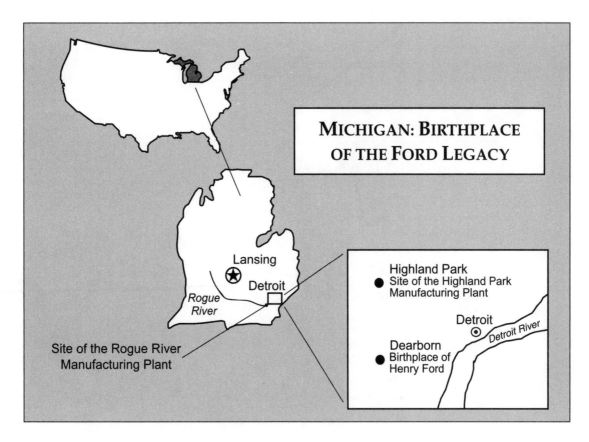

MICHIGAN: BIRTHPLACE OF THE FORD LEGACY

Lansing
Detroit
Rogue River
Site of the Rogue River Manufacturing Plant

Highland Park
Site of the Highland Park Manufacturing Plant
Detroit
Detroit River
Dearborn
Birthplace of Henry Ford

kept the wood box filled from the pile in the adjoining woodshed. Each child had his slate, slate pencil and copybook. [4]

Every morning, school started with song or prayer. Much of the instruction that followed involved rote memory—spelling, enunciation, and pronunciation. Other lessons, and the school environment as a whole, emphasized traditional morality in an effort to ensure that students behaved properly in and outside of school. Biographer Robert Lacey says, "The single-room Dearborn schoolhouse with its dunce's cap, willow cane, and American flag on the wall had provided [Ford] . . . an ideal start in life." [5]

THE MILLER SCHOOL

Henry made slow progress in reading and spelling. Instead, his talents and interest lay in mathematics and science. He was particularly encouraged in these subjects by a teacher named Franklin Ward, who taught at the South Settlement School from 1872 to 1873. In 1873, Ward changed schools, securing a teaching position at the Miller School in a neighboring district. Henry followed, enrolling in the Miller School so that he could continue to study under Ward. There, too, Henry applied himself in his favorite subjects and, under Ward's instruction, became adept at mental arithmetic (doing speedy addition, subtraction, multiplication, and division without counting on his fingers or doodling with pencil and paper).

As a schoolboy, Henry put his mind to work outside the classroom as well. He especially enjoyed exploring mechanics. Biographer Rose Wilder Lane tells of one incident involving his mechanical experimentation:

At the age of seven, Henry Ford began attending the single-room South Settlement School (pictured).

DISCIPLINE IN THE FORD FAMILY

In biographer James Brough's The Ford Dynasty, *Henry Ford describes his mother's disciplinary method.*

"To [Henry], the figure of respected authority was Mother. [Ford says,] 'I was never whipped, but I was punished when I deserved it. . . . I was made to pay the penalty of my misconduct. I was humiliated. Shame cuts more deeply than a whip. Once, when I told a lie, Mother made me suffer the experience of a liar. For a day I was treated with contempt, and I knew I had done a despicable thing. There was no smiling at or glossing over my shortcomings. I learned from her that wrongdoing carries with it its own punishment. There is no escape.'"

In the Ford house, Henry's mother Mary (pictured) was the disciplinarian.

[The Ford family] set out for church as usual. At the hitching-posts, where William Ford tied the horse before going into the church, they met their neighbors, the Bennetts. Will Bennett, a youngster about Henry's age [showed Henry a] . . . watch his grandfather had given to him. . . . "That ain't much," [Henry] scornfully remarked. "It ain't runnin'. . . . I bet I c'n fix it for you." Then he set to work and took out every screw in the mechanism. . . . When at last outraged parental authority descended upon the boys, Henry's Sunday clothes were a wreck, his hands and face were grimy, but he had correctly replaced most of the screws. [6]

Henry's school years also gave him the opportunity to entice his classmates into helping with mechanical projects. One time, Henry and several friends used an old coffee grinder as a base to rig up a small mill that pulverized grain and clay. Another time, they made a steam engine out of metal scraps that worked well enough to explode and injure two of the young engineers.

MARY FORD DIES

On May 17, 1876, when Henry was almost thirteen, his mother had another baby. The infant did not survive, and Mary Ford grew very ill. Twelve days later, Henry's mother also died.

Mary Ford's death devastated her oldest son. In fact, the incident profoundly affected him throughout his life. As Robert Lacey writes, "Henry Ford never forgot the grief and shock of his mother's death. . . . In all manner of ways the adult Henry Ford was to revere his mother's memory with a fervor that amounted to fixation."[7]

A NEW MACHINE

Although saddened by his mother's death, Henry maintained his interest in machines. One machine in particular intrigued him. While riding with his father one day in the family's wagon, the pair came across a neighbor, Fred Reden, who was driving a wagon powered by a steam engine.

Reden's steam engine looked like a railroad locomotive. Steam from boiling water inside the boiler drove a series of six inter-locking gears connected to the axle of the wagon. Although the steam-driven engine made two hundred revolutions a minute, the wagon, loaded down with its huge water tank and a wood-burning stove to heat the water, moved very slowly. Biographer Charles Merz describes the wagon:

> At a bend in the highway there appeared before him [Henry Ford] suddenly the first road vehicle moving under its own power that he had ever seen. It rose in the sunlight, bumping and thundering down the road, like a splendid iron monster. Its heavy sides were a gleaming black. Its huge rollers rumbled ponderously. Smoke shot in a sooty cloud from its thick-set stack.[8]

Henry was fascinated. He asked Reden countless questions about how the engine worked and if it had the power to turn the wheels of threshers, grinders, flour mills, and other farm equipment. After seeing the steam-powered vehicle and asking many questions about it, Henry came to believe that a machine like Reden's could take the place of animals used for labor. Such a machine would be immensely helpful to farmers because it would not require regular food and attention the way animals did. Instead, it could run on firewood. And as long as a farmer maintained his wood supply, he could rely on machines to do the hard work.

MACHINES COME INTO FOCUS

Two other events in 1876 shaped the focus of Henry's next few years. The first was re-

The self-propelled steam engine (pictured) gave rise to internal combustion technology, a lifelong interest for Henry Ford.

ceiving a watch for his thirteenth birthday. The fact that watches seemed to run by themselves intrigued the boy, and he wanted to learn more about how the small machines worked. Says biographer James Brough, "Its [the watch's] importance for him lay not in telling time by it but in his taking it apart and assembling it over and over again until he knew every piece and its function."[9]

The second event began with William Ford's trip to Philadelphia to attend the International Centennial Exposition, a science fair celebrating the hundredth anniversary of the nation's independence. The exposition exhibited the world's newest scientific achievements.

When William Ford returned, he told Henry about the Machine Hall exhibits, which included not only many steam-powered machines but at least seven types of an even newer invention being developed in Germany and France. This invention was an engine that burned gasoline inside a cylinder with a moving plug, or piston. Thus, it was when Ford was thirteen that he first heard of the science that would become his lifelong interest: internal combustion, the burning of fuel inside a machine, rather than water under a boiler to make steam.

Henry's interest in the potential of engines and machines never waned. Once he had finished eighth grade at the Miller School (the highest grade offered in the area), he was able to put that interest to practical use in his work on the farm. One of his duties was to fix machines or tools that did not work. He also kept saws sharpened and mowers and other machinery in good working order.

News of the boy's skill with such repairs spread to other farms, and soon Henry found himself working for his neighbors. Henry thoroughly enjoyed performing such tasks. "Everything he saw moving," says a neighbor of the Fords, "he wanted to experiment with."[10] Biographer Roger Burlingame writes,

> It was usual for [Henry], once he had put the home tools in order, to mount one of the farm horses and ride, bare-

back and barefoot, to the farms of neighbors and fix their things. He . . . seems to have ridden over much of the country, picking up clocks and watches that needed repair, taking them home, working on them into the late night, and returning them better than new.[11]

THE BIG CITY

But even these opportunities did not satisfy Henry's interest in machines. On December 1, 1879, when he was sixteen years old, Henry Ford decided to leave the farm. He had learned all he could there, he thought, and it was time to move on.

At the age of sixteen, Henry Ford moved to Detroit (pictured) to pursue his interest in mechanics.

Henry walked nine miles to Detroit and moved in with his aunt Rebecca. He got a job working for friends of the family, the Flower brothers, James, George, and Thomas. Their factory, Flower Brothers' Machine Shop, made a variety of metal items. According to a fellow worker there, mechanic Frederick Strauss, "They manufactured everything in the line of brass and iron—globe and gate valves, gongs, steam whistles, fire hydrants, and valves for water pipes. . . . They made so many different articles that they had to have all kinds of machines, large and small lathes, and drill presses. . . . They had more machines than workmen in that shop."[12]

The next year, when he was seventeen, Ford took another step toward being on his own. He left Flower Brothers, moved out of his aunt Rebecca's house, and became an engineer's apprentice with shipbuilders at the Detroit Dry Dock Company. Here, he thought, he could learn about the iron and steel industry.

However, finding that his Dry Dock earnings of $2.50 a week would not pay his room rent, which was $3.50 a week, he took a second job in the evening, repairing watches. According to biographers Peter Collier and David Horowitz, "For a time he thought of going into the watchmaking business, but changed his mind after calculating that he would have to sell 600,000 watches a year simply to break even."[13]

BACK TO DEARBORN

During the first two years that Henry lived in Detroit, he returned to Dearborn in the summers to help out with the work on his father's farm. He also continued to do the same types of repair and mechanical work he had done for his neighbors before he went to the city. At the end of his third year in Detroit, Ford considered himself a qualified mechanic and took a steady job in Dearborn working for his father's neighbor, John Gleason.

Gleason owned a steam engine, so Henry was excited about his new employment. Gleason, too, was glad to be working with Henry Ford. One of his previous employees had quit after being frightened by the noisy steam engine. Henry, though, was not intimidated by the machine. Not only did Henry keep the steam engine in good working condition, but he also took it out around the county and operated it when Gleason was hired to perform custom farm jobs, such as threshing, for his neighbors.

That arrangement lasted only a summer, but it worked out well. Henry Ford later wrote,

> I was paid three dollars a day and had eighty-three days of steady work. I traveled from farm to farm, and I threshed our own and the neighbors' clover, hauled loads, cut cornstalks, ground feed, sawed wood. It was hard work. I had to fire [the steam engine] myself and the fuel most generally was old fence rails, though it would burn coal the few times coal was to be had. I became immensely fond of that machine. . . . I have never been better satisfied with myself than I was when I guided it over the rough country roads.[14]

Growing Up Near Detroit

Henry Ford grew up in rural Michigan near the busy, industrialized lakeside city of Detroit. In Ford: The Times, the Man, the Company, *biographer Allan Nevins discusses the role Detroit and industrialization played in the life of Henry Ford.*

"A farm youth reared on the outskirts of Detroit could not escape the influences of the time and place. As Henry Ford entered childhood just after the Civil War, he could sometimes see on the horizon to the southeast a haze made by the heavy smoke of the freighters constantly passing between Lake Erie on the south and Lakes St. Clair and Huron on the north; he could see to the east the faint but ever-denser smudge of Detroit's numerous small mills, factories, and machine shops. . . .

Even little Dearbornville, the Fords' own village, had known in the 1840's a touch of the coming industrial era; a description of it [Dearborn] enumerates 'a sawmill with double saws, flour mills . . . seven stores, two smitheries, and a foundry for iron propelled by water power, a physician, and about sixty families.'"

Henry Ford as an adolescent. Henry Ford grew up near the industrialized city of Detroit.

The Ideal Job

After his summer job with Gleason, Ford went on to another mechanic's job. He became an area representative for the machinery manufacturer Westinghouse, demonstrating its steam engines to farmers throughout southern Michigan. He was also responsible for fixing the en-

gines he sold. Says one writer, Ford went "traveling around the countryside with a bag of tools to operate and service the company's machine."[15]

His work as a mechanic put Ford in regular contact with farmers, and he became interested in their problems and concerns. As he listened to their tales of the hard times on farms, where production had been boosted by new farming technology, he formed opinions that often matched theirs. The government should print more money, he thought. The railroads charged too much to haul their goods. These were political views he continued to hold and discuss for years to come.

A Down-Home Courtship

In 1885, toward the end of his job with Westinghouse, Ford met Clara Jane Bryant, the popular oldest daughter of a Greenfield, Michigan, farmer, at a New Year's dance. She was nineteen, three years younger than Ford, but much more socially involved. It was another year before the two met again.

At her second meeting with Ford, Bryant took an interest in him. He seemed to her more mature and original than other young men she knew. She said she was impressed because

> He was so different from all the other young men I had known. You know how they are, talk about how good the music is and all that sort of thing. He didn't. I remember he showed me a watch that he'd fixed himself . . . and he explained how he'd done it. I remember going home and telling [my family] how sensible he was, how serious-minded.[16]

As for Ford, he had found Clara Bryant interesting at the first meeting. Thus, when she showed interest in him, he made a special effort to maintain a good impression. He took dancing lessons and wrote her letters.

The Ford family liked Clara also. His sister Margaret thought that Clara's well-balanced sociability and charm seemed like a good match for Henry's impractical and visionary personality. William Ford hoped that marrying a farm girl would keep Henry from returning to Detroit and his obsession with machines. But, as Collier and Horowitz write, that was not to be:

> When he saw that his son was in love William Ford tried one last time to set the hook that would make him a farmer, by offering him an eighty-acre parcel [of land] he had acquired a few years earlier . . . . There was a little house and thick stands of harvestable hardwoods. Henry quickly moved in, set up a sawmill and began cutting and milling the black oak, maple and elm. To William Ford's dismay, however, he also immediately built a shop and resumed his tinkering, this time with gasoline engines as well as steam.[17]

Life on the Farm

Henry Ford courted Clara Bryant for two and a half years before he proposed. They married at the Bryant farm on April 11, 1888. Immediately afterward, they moved into the small wooden house on Ford's eighty acres for the beginning of their married life.

Both Henry and Clara found the cabin inadequate for their needs, however. Thus, only a few weeks after their wedding, they began planning the construction of a nicer house. Clara designed the new house, complete with a veranda and ornately carved wooden, or "gingerbread," trimming in the gables. It was built within the year.

The couple was happy, but they had very different personalities. A simple farm life suited Clara. From the outset, she valued economy and security. She handled the couple's finances and kept a small garden. Henry, on the other hand, liked quiet time in his workshop. To earn a living, he sold lumber and raised livestock. During

LEAVING THE FLOWER BROTHERS' MACHINE SHOP

Henry Ford believed that nothing, not materials or time, should be wasted. Thus, the wastefulness he observed at the Flower Brothers' Machine Shop irritated him and ultimately prompted him to leave. In this excerpt from her book Henry Ford's Own Story, *author Rose Wilder Lane describes the wastefulness at Flower Brothers.*

"The mammoth shop of James Flower & Co., with its great force of a hundred mechanics, became familiar to him [Henry Ford]; it shrank from the huge proportions it had at first assumed in his eyes. He began to see imperfections in its system and to be annoyed by them.

'See here,' he said one day to the man who worked beside him. 'Nothing's ever made twice alike in this place. We waste a lot of time and material assembling these engines. That piston rod'll have to be made over, it won't fit the cylinder.'

'Oh, well, I guess we do the best we can,' the other man said. 'It won't take long to fit it.' It was the happy-go-lucky method of factories in the seventies [1870s].

Men were shifted from job to job to suit the whim of the foreman. . . . Parts were cast, recast, filed down to fit other parts. Scrap iron accumulated in the corner of the shop. A piece of work was abandoned half finished in order to make up time on another order, delayed by some accident. By today's [1923] standards it was a veritable helter-skelter, from which the finished machines somehow emerged, at a fearful cost in wasted time and labor.

When Henry was switched from one piece of work to another . . . or sent to get a needed tool that was missing, he knew his time was being wasted."

Henry Ford sought ways to replace the horse-drawn plow (pictured) with more efficient engine-powered machines.

the summers, when the neighboring farmers needed extra help, Ford continued to work with steam engines and took on occasional jobs such as setting up engines for the farm machinery business Buckeye Harvester Company.

Despite his land and marriage, Ford's early interests remained important. He continued searching for a way to make farmwork easier. Traveling to Detroit on repair or sales assignments for Buckeye Harvester, he often considered the prospect of replacing farm animals with machines. He later wrote, "I felt perfectly certain that horses, considering all the bother of attending them and the expense of feeding, did not earn their keep. . . . To lift farm drudgery off flesh and blood and lay it on steel and motors has been my most constant ambition." [18]

2 Better than Steam

Although happy with his marriage, Henry Ford was restless living on his farm. His work with engines and machines had to be secondary, taking a backseat to his farm work. In his spare time, he began reading about the internal combustion engine that his father had viewed in 1876 at the Philadelphia Centennial Exposition. Then, in his workshop on the farm, he began trying to make one. "The gasoline engine interested me," he later wrote, "and I followed its progress."[19]

THE SILENT OTTO

That engine, which had been invented in Germany by Nikolaus August Otto and his collaborator Gottlieb Daimler, was called the "silent Otto." It operated on an explosive mixture of gasoline and air compressed in a cylinder. When the mixture was ignited, it exploded and moved a piston past a valve that allowed the smoke to escape. A new supply of fuel was then taken in for the next explosion. A piston rod transmitted the motion of the piston to gears connected to shafts and axles.

In 1891, Ford's part-time employer, Buckeye Harvester Company, called him to De-

troit to look at a model of the silent Otto. When Ford saw for himself the compact little engine powered not by steam but by gasoline, he became convinced of its value for practical purposes. He felt certain that he could make a gasoline engine propel itself and turn the wheels of the vehicle that supported it, something like the steam engine belonging to Fred Reden.

The biggest problem Ford anticipated in making such a vehicle was finding a simple way to ignite the mixture of gasoline and air inside the cylinder. Looking around Detroit for an answer to this question, he became interested in the new electrical industries. Ford hoped to use electricity to ignite a spark in the cylinder.

A BIG MOVE

In his search, Ford visited the Edison Illuminating Company, which generated electricity for the city of Detroit. That visit convinced him that he needed to leave the farm and learn more about electricity. Thus, he applied for and got a job at the Edison Illuminating Company. The salary of forty-five dollars a month, Ford said later, "was more money than the farm was bringing me, and

I had decided to get away from farm life anyway. The timber had all been cut."[20]

Ford took the job with the Edison Illuminating Company without consulting his wife. To him, there were few complications. He came straight home and told Clara they were moving to Detroit.

Henry Ford was not in the habit of asking his wife for advice, so Clara did not argue, even though she did not want to leave the house she had designed and move far away from her family. According to biographer James Brough, "Leaving the farm [Clara Ford] said, 'nearly broke my heart,' but to do otherwise would be a breach of faith."[21] Thus, in the late summer of 1891 the Fords moved from their square house in Dearborn to rented lodgings in Detroit.

WORKING FOR EDISON ILLUMINATING COMPANY

Ford's employment with the Edison Illuminating Company was his first opportunity to be a leader, and he proved to be good at it. He was put in charge of routine maintenance. His crew cleaned the cylinders leading to the turbines and kept the ball bearings oiled and running smoothly. Their duties were a team activity that brought out Ford's leadership abilities. Biographer

Machinists illuminate a lamp at the Edison Illuminating Company. Henry Ford got a job at Edison in 1891.

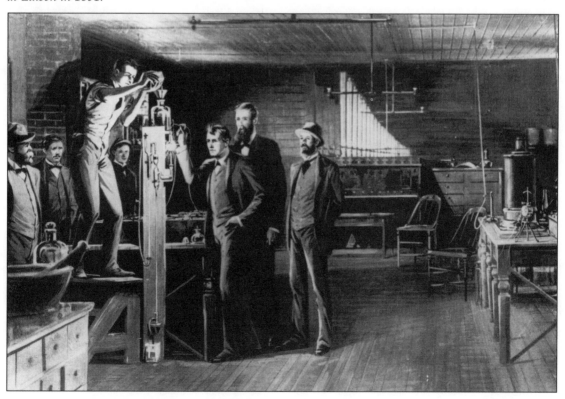

Robert Lacey notes that "Ford appears to have had the knack of running a trouble-free shop. He managed to simplify things that could have been complicated . . . and his superiors at the Edison Company rewarded him with wage rises [raises], promotions, and a certain freedom."[22]

One of the freedoms the Edison job allowed Ford was unoccupied time between duties. Ford generally spent this time in a break room talking with other employees. As the weeks went on, the men shared their enthusiasm and ideas about mechanics. One topic, the Otto engines, came up often.

Over time, Ford and the other men began to understand more about how the Otto engine worked and how it delivered power. Before long, they began making engines of their own. Sometimes, they tried to duplicate what they had read about the Otto, following diagrams in the *American Machinist* magazine. Other times, they struck out on their own, designing new kinds of connections for the pistons, piston rods, and gears. The engines they made were mostly impractical. However, they did develop a sense of companionship and common purpose and an appreciation of the skills and abilities each brought to the tasks.

BREAKTHROUGH

In 1893, two years after the Fords moved to Detroit, Henry Ford turned thirty. As he and Clara awaited the birth of their first child, the couple moved into a new home. On November 6, 1893, their only child, a son, was born. The Fords named him Edsel, after researcher and scientist Edsel

Ruddiman, a childhood friend who had married Henry Ford's sister Margaret.

Meanwhile, Ford and the men at Edison continued working on their gasoline engine. They still had not worked out the problem of ignition, getting the electrical spark to the gasoline in a way that would initiate an even, regular explosion inside the cylinder without blowing up the engine. It was six more weeks before Ford finally thought he had the solution.

That day, he came into the house to ask Clara to help him test the device. With the baby sleeping nearby, Clara dripped gasoline into Henry's motor while he touched a loose wire to the household electrical current. Luckily, the gasoline explosion did what it was meant to do. It exploded inside the cylinder. The first working model of a Ford motor had stood the test.

Within a few weeks, Ford was promoted at the Edison Company and moved from his substation to the company's main power-house. He was given a raise and the title of chief engineer.

Although the promotion, by changing his place of work, eliminated the breaks he had been enjoying with his fellow employees at the substation, Ford's success with the gasoline engine experiment gave him new energy. He moved his tools to a shed behind the Fords' new home, and his friends soon followed. The group that eventually settled into serious motor building was George Cato, an electrician, and two mechanics, James W. Bishop and Edward "Spider" Huff.

Ford's new workstation and the opportunities it brought also introduced him

A replica of Henry Ford's first workshop, where he built his first gasoline-powered engine.

to two men whose ideas urged him on. The first was a student named Oliver Barthel. Ford met Barthel when he was teaching a machinist's class for the YMCA. The second man was Charles Brady King, Barthel's employer, who also was building a self-propelled machine, which he called a "horseless carriage." Over the next two years, King and Barthel's enthusiasm and their work on their own engines became a source of competition for Ford.

A PERSISTENT GROUP

Inspired and excited, Ford spent most of his spare time building his motor. As biographer Charles Merz writes,

> [Making a motor] was tedious, exacting, lonesome work. It needed money: Ford had no money save a weekly wage of eleven dollars and a small income from the farm he had rented to a neighbor. It needed care and ingenuity: Ford came to the task each night after a workday of ten hours. It needed raw materials that would stand up under a variety of experiments: Ford worked with junk; he built his cylinders out of the exhaust pipe of a discarded steam engine which he had purchased as old iron. . . . Ford did not have blueprints of the gas engines that had been invented. Nor did he build an engine like the gas engine he had once repaired.[23]

Ford's effort to build his own motor was spurred on by the knowledge that, even once he had built it, he still had a long way to go to transmit the motor's power to the wheels of a vehicle. Others were far ahead of him in using gasoline engines for transportation. Vehicles called automobiles were

Henry Ford wheels the quadricycle out of his workshop.

already in commercial production in France. Cars had been built in Germany by Gottleib Daimler and Karl Benz. And in Springfield, Massachusetts, the American team of Charles and Frank Duryea built a working automobile in 1893.

By the beginning of 1896, though, Ford and his group of mechanics from the Edison substation were successful enough at building their motor to try to put the experimental engine up for sale.

The money the men made from these sales gave them what they needed to connect their motor to wheels.

Their work seemed to progress slowly, however. That same year, Barthel and King finished their "horseless carriage," which weighed thirteen hundred pounds and went five miles an hour. A little later, in Springfield, Charles and Frank Duryea

tested a vehicle that reached a speed of six and six-tenths miles per hour. Ford and his fellow machinists began to worry that they were falling further and further behind.

THE QUADRICYCLE

However slow their progress, Ford, Cato, Bishop, and Huff had solidified into a team. And as a team, they concluded that King and Barthel's wagon was too heavy. Thus, the men decided to reduce the weight of their vehicle; a lighter weight would not require so much power to move. They also hoped that it would be cheaper to build something lighter. With the lighter weight as a goal, the men mounted their motor on two bicycle frames. They named this vehicle the "quadricycle."

FORD'S FIRST CAR

According to biographer Robert Lacey in Ford: The Men and the Machine, *Ford's first car, the quadricycle, was too big to fit through the door of his workshop. Thus, moving it onto the street for a test drive required a few adjustments to the garage in which the vehicle was built.*

"Finally, in the small hours of June 4, 1896, it [the Quadricycle] was complete. Clara was there—she often stayed up to keep her husband company—and so was Jim Bishop, one of the comrades from work. Jim was to be the outrider on the first expedition, escorting Henry on his bicycle.... But as the two men readied themselves to push the Quadricycle out into the street, Henry Ford realized the most ridiculous mistake. He and his helpers had been so intent on building up the Quadricycle over the past weeks, testing its two cylinders and fitting all the parts together, that they had forgotten they were doing this with the aim of one day taking the machine out through the door—and the door was only a standard one.

At this point, doubtless, Henry Ford would have brought the entire shed and the rest of Bagley Avenue crashing down if he had to. He got an axe, demolished the door frame, knocked out several courses of bricks, and finally the machine was free. Clara came out to wish the car Godspeed [success], with a shawl over her head and an umbrella, since there was a light rain falling. Henry turned on the current from the battery, adjusted the gasoline, and placed his thumb and finger over the device that he used as a choke. He turned over the flywheel, the engine shuddered, and the Quadricycle came to life."

Henry Ford sits atop his first car, the quadricycle.

The quadricycle made its first test run on June 4, 1896. Thanks to its lightweight frame, it reached a speed of twenty miles per hour, fifteen more than that of King's wagon. Ford describes the quadricycle in his autobiography:

This first car had something of the appearance of a buggy. . . . The car would hold two people, the seat being suspended on posts and the body on elliptical springs. There were two speeds —one of ten and the other of twenty miles per hour—obtained by shifting the belt, which was done by a clutch lever in front of the driving seat. Thrown forward, the lever put in the high speed; thrown back the low speed; with the lever upright the engine could run free [idle]. To start the car it was necessary to turn the motor over by hand with the clutch free. To stop the car one simply released the clutch and applied the foot brake. There was no reverse. . . . The wheels were twenty-eight-inch wire bicycle wheels with rubber tires. . . . A tank under the seat held three gallons of gasoline which was fed to the motor through a small pipe and a mixing valve.[24]

FORD'S FIRST COMPANY

Ford's quadricycle was noisy enough and unusual enough to draw crowds wherever he went with it. Among those who paid attention to Ford's ideas about transportation by gasoline-powered engines was the Fords' next-door neighbor, William Maybury, the mayor of Detroit. Maybury's interest led him to supply Ford with small amounts of cash to work on improvements for his motor.

Ford soon realized that he needed more than one investor, though. To gain support, he visited William Murphy, who was part owner of the Edison Illuminating Company. After taking Murphy for a drive in the quadricycle, Ford was successful in getting Murphy's support as well.

As a result, Murphy and Maybury, along with some owners of the Detroit Dry Dock Company, formed Detroit's first car-manufacturing company. They called it the Detroit Automobile Company. On August 5, 1899, with Ford as their mechanical superintendent and car designer, they announced that they would make cars for sale. Believing that the company would be profitable, Henry Ford, whose job at the automobile company gave him some stock and a small salary, resigned from Edison.

The Detroit Automobile Company established a car-manufacturing site, and Ford went right to work on building a car. Barely six months later, on February 4, 1900, the company put out its first product, a shiny black delivery wagon. The delivery wagon was quickly considered a marvel. A *Detroit News-Tribune* reporter called it "the newest and most perfect of forces . . . rushing along at the rate of 25 miles an hour."[25]

EARLY FAILURE

During the next nine months, however, the company's success did not realize Ford's

CLARA AND EDSEL

For a short time in 1901, Clara Bryant Ford kept a diary, showing her and her husband's devotion to their young son, Edsel. This excerpt from the diary is reprinted in Robert Lacey's Ford: The Men and the Machine.

"January 11, 1901
Snowed all day. Edsel got soaking wet. He and Grandpa [William Ford] played checkers. Edsel cheated awful and beat every game. Went to bed so full of laughs he could not say his prayers.

Sat. January 12
Went downtown, got Edsel shoes and leggings. Went into Sheaffer's [department] store to hear the music. After supper we tried to learn [teach] Grandpa to play cards.

Sun. January 13
Edsel and I went to S[unday] School. . . . Came home, had dinner, then Henry fixed Edsel's old sleigh to take him coasting [sledding], but Edsel would not go, said sleigh was no good. He was sent up stairs for punishment for his pride. He was sorry.

January 19
Henry bought Edsel new coaster [sled]."

hopes for making money. The production costs for manufacturing twelve of their new cars went eighty-six thousand dollars over budget. Workmen complained that Ford's sketches were not good enough for them to work from efficiently. In turn, Ford complained that he had too little time and authority to improve his car design and make a car more useful for the buyers. In order to avoid further losses, the company dissolved in November 1900.

Some biographers contend that the failure of the Detroit Automobile Company had a lot to do with Henry Ford's unreadiness to adapt to his new job and the responsibilities it gave him. Says Robert Lacey, "Henry had not yet come to terms

with the new dimension he was working in. He was no longer a power station supervisor, fiddling with engines in a back room as a hobby. . . . The Detroit Automobile Company had offered him a chance to catch up, or even to get ahead of the [car-making] game—and Henry had muffed it." [26]

The end of the Detroit Automobile Company put Ford out of work. So, he and his family moved in with Ford's sister Jane and his father, William Ford, who had retired from farming after suffering a stroke. Initially, the arrangement seemed to work well. Seven-year-old Edsel enjoyed spending time with his grandfather, and Ford was busy working out a new idea, a racing

Alexander Winton (driver) races around the track in 1901.

car. In later years, however, Ford implied that the living situation was contentious at times.

BUILDING UP SPEED

Despite the dissolution of the Detroit Automobile Company, William Murphy continued to support Ford. He rode in Ford's experimental cars and listened to Ford's enthusiastic discussion of ways to improve his engines. Soon, Murphy became convinced that Ford could build speedier engines than the other carmakers around the country. Believing that one of the reasons for the Detroit Automobile Company's failure was a lack of advertising, and that the buying public would be more likely to

purchase something showcased in competition, Murphy encouraged Ford to work on a race car.

With the financial and motivational help of Murphy, Ford and his three team members spent the next several months building a race car and designing what would become the key to its speed. Their device, an induction coil encapsulated in a little porcelain insulating case, was the first spark plug. Replacing the uninsulated sparker of the quadricycle, the new spark plug reliably delivered an electric spark to the fuel.

Ford and his friends looked forward to an opportunity to test their spark plug and to prove that lighter cars would travel faster. Their opportunity came when Alexander Winton, a carmaker from Cleveland, Ohio, decided to stage a race near Detroit on October 10, 1901. The race would fulfill Ford's need for advertising to the buying public. Says biographer Roger Burlingame, "Henry was, at this time, determined to enter track races as a means of publicity. . . . He did not believe that capacity for high speed added to the value of a car. But he knew that, at that particular moment in automotive history, breaking records at track races was the way to celebrity."[27]

Winton, however, was interested in speed. He hoped to beat the world speed record set in 1901 by Henri Fournier of France, who drove a mile in 1 minute 6.8 seconds. To accomplish this goal, Winton's backers and race organizers planned a ten-lap, ten-mile race in Grosse Pointe, Michigan, just north of Detroit.

Winton's hopes were unfulfilled. Rather than allow Winton to break the speed record, the race boosted Ford's celebrity. In the middle of the race, Winton's car overheated, emitting a cloud of blue smoke. Ford's car had no trouble, although as an inexperienced driver, Ford was unable to make close turns. Thus, he lost ground on the first five laps. In the seventh lap, though, Ford pulled ahead. To the delight of the Detroit-based crowd, he maintained his lead. "All Detroit was now convinced that a motor-car could race,"[28] commented writer Upton Sinclair.

THE SHORT-LIVED HENRY FORD COMPANY

Among the spectators at the Ford-Winton race were William Murphy and four other Detroit Automobile Company investors. Realizing the potential of Ford's racing car, they approached Ford and proposed a new car-manufacturing corporation. After their experience with what they considered Ford's lack of commitment to the Detroit Automobile Company, Murphy and his partners wanted to make sure that the control of the new company, its finances, and its products rested solely with them. Thus, they hired Ford as chief engineer and paid him in stock. They agreed to provide money for materials and labor to produce cars according to his design. In return, Ford agreed to let them call their corporation the Henry Ford Company and to produce salable cars. If he did not produce such a car, Ford would be fired and have to give up the plans for his racer.

In fact, Ford did not complete his side of the agreement. He was more interested in his own plans than in designs for someone else's company. Four months later, Murphy found that Ford was secretly at work on a new racer of his own. As agreed, Ford was dismissed with a nine-hundred dollar settlement and the Henry Ford Company dissolved.

THE ARROW AND THE 999

Undeterred, Ford continued to talk about his cars and his dream of manufacturing cars. In the next few weeks, he got financial advice and encouragement from a young hardware merchant named James Couzens. He also got some money from Tom Cooper, a racing driver he had met at the Winton race. And he enlisted the help of a well-educated Welshman, Childe Harold Wills,

BARNEY OLDFIELD WINS THE RACE

In 1902, Barney Oldfield raced Henry Ford's car, the 999, in an official competition. The story of his and the car's performance is narrated in an article titled "The Rise of Henry Ford" that was published in the Literary Digest *on February 24, 1917.*

"[On the day of the race, October 25, 1902,] Ford and [friend Tom] Cooper, tense with anxiety, went over the car thoroughly and coached Oldfield for the last time. [Ford's friend and promoter James] Couzens, hiding his nervousness under a bland, confident manner, gathered his group of business men and took them into the stand. The free-for-all [race] was called. Half a dozen cars were entered. When they had found their places in the field, Barney Oldfield settled himself in his seat, firmly grasped the two-handed tiller which steered the mighty car, and remarked, 'Well, this chariot may kill me, but they'll say afterward that I was going some when the car went over the bank.'

Ford cranked the engine, and the race was on.

Oldfield, his long hair snapping in the wind, shot from the midst of the astounded field like a bullet. He did not dare look around; he merely clung to the tiller and gave that car all the power it had. At the end of the first half he was far in the lead and gaining fast.

The crowd, astounded, hysterical with excitement, saw him streak past the grand stand a quarter of a mile ahead of the nearest car following. On the second lap he still gained. Grasping the tiller, never for a second relaxing that terrific speed, he spun around the course again, driving as if the field was at his heels.

He roared in at the finish, a full half mile ahead of the nearest car, in a three-mile race."

Henry Ford stands next to his 999 racer. Barney Oldfield (seated) drove the vehicle to victory in 1902.

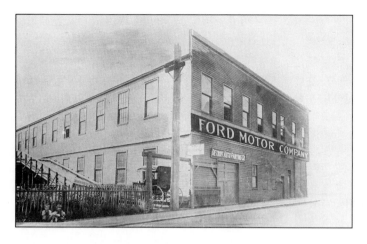

The Ford Motor Company building. The emergence of the Ford Motor Company revolutionized the American car-making industry.

who was a professional draftsman. With the benefit of Wills's ability to commit designs to paper, Ford designed a reliable transmission for his racer.

Ford and Wills finished two racers, the Arrow and the 999, in time for a race scheduled at Grosse Pointe in October 1902. These were noisy and powerful cars with seventy-horsepower engines. The huge engines were placed in front of the driver's seat, rather than under it as in previous models.

Afraid to drive in that race, Ford convinced bicyclist Barney Oldfield to take the wheel of the 999. Oldfield won the race, doing more than seventy miles per hour. Writes Burlingame, Ford's racer "broke all records . . . over a three-mile course, with the daredevil Barney Oldfield driving. This time the news went round the world, and it was an ignoramus indeed who did not recognize the name of Henry Ford."[29]

ANOTHER INVESTMENT

Winning the 1902 Grosse Pointe race brought fame to Henry Ford, but designing race cars would not earn him a living. Racers were only toys that wealthy people used sporadically for entertainment. To make money, Ford was beginning to realize, he needed to build a reliable and useful car. To do that, he needed an efficient and well-planned factory.

The idea of a factory also began to interest James Couzens and wealthy coal supplier Alexander Y. Malcomson. On June 16, 1903, Malcomson, Couzens, and several other investors pooled enough money to build a factory to assemble Ford's cars and hire workers.

Malcomson, Ford, and their partners called this new company the Ford Motor Company. Together, Ford, as designer, and Malcomson, as director, held 51 percent of the company's stock, which they split evenly between them. The other partners bought the rest.

Ford calculated that the Ford Motor Company could assemble 650 cars at the rate of fifteen cars a day and sell each of them for $150 more than it cost for labor and supplies. This plan would assure each investor a return on his money. Thus, Henry

Ford's idea for an efficient automobile factory touched off the car-making business in the United States. As biographer Roger Burlingame says, "The deal [he made with Malcomson] ended in changing the face of America."[30]

THE MODEL A

Ford and Couzens were personally involved in accomplishing the company's first task: remodeling a building donated by one of the investors to create a factory that suited their production plans. They cleared enough floor space for the fifteen assembly stations and the supply bins for small parts. They also built an unloading dock for the delivery of the motors and other large parts from the suppliers. Biographer Allan Nevins writes, "All spring Ford and Couzens . . . worked like galley-slaves to make [the factory] ready; all summer and fall they labored with the frenzy of harvest-hands racing a storm. . . . Sometimes [they worked] . . . twelve or sixteen hours daily for seven days a week."[31]

Once the car-making began, other investors took specific roles that matched their talents. C. Harold Wills designed the Ford trademark, still in use today, with its graceful capital "F" and helped produce a two-cylinder engine to increase power and reduce vibration. John and Horace Dodge, two investors and excellent machinists, produced the motors.

Ford and Couzens also took on jobs that used their skills. According to Nevins, "From the outset Ford was in charge of production, Couzens of business affairs. On the factory floor Ford was supreme; in the offices Couzens oversaw the book-keeping, wrote letters, paid bills, collected moneys due, and, after mid-November, supervised sales."[32]

The Ford Motor Company's first car, called the Model A, was priced at $850. At the end of three weeks of assembly, though, not one car was purchased. By that time, the company's cash balance was down to less than $500. The first sale, however, to Dr. E. Pfennig, a Chicago dentist, made the company a $223.63 profit. Ford, Malcomson, and the other investors were finally making money off the automobile. "From [then] onwards," says Lacey, "[the Ford Motor Company's] cash flow went one way only."[33]

3 Cars from A to T

The Ford Motor Company's Model A was a stylish automobile. With an eight-horsepower engine, both forward and reverse gears, and twenty-eight-inch wheels with wooden spokes, it promised better performance than the products of most other manufacturers. And orders came in. By May 1904, the Ford Motor Company had sold its first 658 cars. In the months that followed, an average of six hundred cars was ordered per month. Profits, as planned, were $150 per car. Assembly proceeded, and at the end of the year, the profits were divided up among the stockholders. Ford's share, as one-fourth owner and chief engineer, came to $25,000.

NEW DRIVE AND PERSONAL LOSS

Almost as soon as Ford received his first check, he moved his family into a home of their own. The move and the financial success transformed Henry Ford. As vice president of a company with unprecedented profits, he became self-confident and held himself more erect than ever. These changes were apparent in an official photograph taken of Ford in 1904. As biographer Robert Lacey writes,

With his moustache shaved off, . . . he looks rather younger and fresher [in this photograph than in earlier ones]. He obviously has a good many miles left in him.

But in another sense, Henry Ford looks completely different, and the difference lies in small things; in the eyes,

The famous 1904 portrait of Henry Ford, referred to by biographer Robert Lacey.

GUESTS FROM ENGLAND

One of the first people to give a boost to Henry Ford's auto-making ego was an Englishman named Percival Perry who wanted to sell Ford cars in Great Britain. In 1905, Perry was the houseguest of Henry Ford. In Ford: The Men and the Machine, *biographer Robert Lacey describes that visit.*

"Since business was the object of his visit, [Percival Perry] started off with John Gray, the president of the [Ford Motor] company. . . .

'Well,' said Gray, when the Englishman had explained his mission, 'I guess you'll have to see Henry,' and he put Perry on a streetcar to the Piquette Avenue plant. There the Englishman met [designer] Harold Wills, dressed in greasy overalls, as well as Henry Ford, who genially invited Perry and his wife to come and stay in his own home while they were in Detroit.

The Fords still occupied modest quarters. They had plans to build in one of the prestigious new developments out along Woodward Avenue, but for the time being, they were in a rented home on Harper Avenue, not far from the Piquette plant, and the accommodation was cramped when there were guests in the house. Perry had to race the twelve-year-old Edsel to the bathroom every morning. . . .

Percival Perry took to Henry Ford. The carmaker had an unmistakable streak of genius, he decided. . . . Perry thought he could trust Henry, that he was 'a man to whom you would give your last penny.'"

in the crisp clothes, in the set of the jaw. It is a professional portrait, of course, cleverly lit, designed to make him look good. But there is something more, a sense of power and assurance that comes from Henry himself. Suddenly, and for the first time, Henry Ford looks as he was to look for the rest of his life, no longer Henry the shiftless, Henry the tinkerer, Henry the moonlighter, but Henry Ford the successful businessman, Henry Ford the car maker.[34]

Before the end of that year, however, Ford's living situation changed again. His father's health worsened, and Ford's sister Jane could no longer care for him. So, William Ford moved into the new home of Clara, Henry, and Edsel.

William and Henry Ford did not get along, however. And when William died a little more than three months later, on March 8, 1905, Ford's relief was obvious. "Henry," biographer James Brough says, "was liberated from the frustrations of the past."[35]

With a burst of creativity, Ford and Wills began constantly coming up with new and improved features to incorporate into their cars. It seemed that Ford had a renewed sense of his ability to feel his way to better motor design. This ability energized his fellow engineers. During this time, C. Harold Wills and "Spider" Huff, his friend from Edison Illuminating Company, came up with a cheap, sturdy, and even more reliable carburetor to mix the air and gasoline so that the Model A engine ran more smoothly.

Author Anne Jardim writes, "He [Ford] was a charismatic leader . . . and men worked willingly for [him]."[36] In fact, three hundred men were now employed by the Ford Motor Company, and they were making twenty-five cars a day. The company was supplying a sales force of 450 agencies across the continent. July 1905 closed a full year of profits for the Ford Motor Company.

THREE NEW CAR MODELS

In its second year of operation, the Ford Motor Company produced for sale three new cars. Following the alphabetical pattern begun with the Model A, it presented Models B, C, and F.

By building several models offering different amenities to be sold simultaneously at different prices, the company's partners hoped to maximize their profits by appealing to a larger number of car buyers. The Model B, the largest and most expensive model at $2,000, had a four-cylinder motor and appealed to the wealthy. Model C, the least expensive at $800, was designed to appeal to buyers who wanted stylish cars but could not afford the Model B. Model C had two seats that hung close to the ground and white spokes in the wheels. And Model F, at a medium price of $1,000,

The moderately priced Model F (pictured) was one of three cars produced in the Ford Motor Company's second year.

had flashier trimmings on the hood and fancier door handles than Model C.

The sale of three cars at different prices, however, drove an ideological wedge between Ford and his chief backer Alexander Malcomson, as each man began to think ahead to the next cars. Ford was leaning toward an unconventional approach to the automobile business, selling more cars to more ordinary people at lower prices. As his motivation, says Lacey, there was a deep desire to get ahead, to build his success. There was also his background on the farm and his ingrained distrust of the rich, the opinions Ford had formed during his years of fixing Westinghouse machines. As Lacey writes, "[His attitude] was partly, to be sure, plain prejudice, the country-boy suspicion of the upper crust—and it was also . . . a matter of sheer ambition."[37]

The more traditional Malcomson, on the other hand, thought the way other car manufacturers of the time did. He believed that selling fewer expensive cars to wealthier customers was the route to success and profit. In fact, Malcomson's thinking was not without merit. At the beginning of the twentieth century, automobiles were indeed expensive and reserved for the wealthy. As Lacey writes, "From 1903 to 1907, the proportion of cars costing more than $1,375 [at a time when teachers earned an average annual salary of $850] showed significant annual increases, for as the car habit caught on, it was the rich who came in faster."[38]

FORD AND MALCOMSON

The difference in the two men's approaches did not become apparent immediately. It was not until the company began work on the Model K that the difference of opinion caused problems. The Model K was a six-cylinder car, the kind of grand luxury touring car that would appeal to the wealthy. The company was already assembling twenty-five of the cheaper Models B, C, and F a day, and sales were good. Malcomson foresaw proportionately higher profits from selling the more expensive Model Ks, and he began to push for the introduction of the Model K as soon as possible.

Ford, however, had a different idea. He and Couzens had been discussing building a car that would be affordable for most Americans. With the help of Wills, Ford and Couzens devised a simple production plan and an argument for its introduction. Building Model Ks at this time, they argued, was not cost effective because they would have to renovate their factory to accommodate its production. Furthermore, it would take many hours of work at the Dodge brothers' plant (where the motors were made) to install the machinery to manufacture all of the Model K's luxury details. Instead, they said, the company should build simpler cars and sell them at $400 each.

The ideological conflict between Ford and Malcomson soon became apparent to the stockholders. While Malcomson insisted on moving forward with production of the Model K, Ford became insistent on entering the more affordable market. As the argument heated, the various stockholders began to take sides. Couzens sided with Ford. The Dodge brothers, unhappy about giving up the profits promised by sales of the Model K, sided with Malcomson.

PROGRESS TOWARD ASSEMBLY-LINE MANUFACTURING

During production of the Model N, the Ford Motor Company began experimenting with mass production, trying to produce large numbers of identical cars quickly. According to biographer Robert Lacey, in Ford: The Men and the Machine, *mass-producing cars was difficult at first.*

"Mass production was a long-established tradition in American industry: Singer sewing machines, McCormick reapers, the small arms manufacturing of [gun maker] Samuel Colt. Now Ford and Couzens were proposing to apply mass production to the car industry for the first time. . . . [Another car manufacturer] Ransom E. Olds had managed to turn out 5,000 of his 'Merry Oldsmobiles' in 1903 before his backers took his company upmarket [appealed to wealthy buyers]. In 1906, Ford and Couzens were aiming at double that.

They soon discovered that mass production was easier said than done. In the absence of the moving assembly line which was, eventually, to prove the secret to smooth production of cars in bulk, they had to go for sheer weight of numbers: more workstations, more men, more machines. They had more than doubled their own capacity, thanks to the workshops of the Ford Manufacturing Company, but when Model N production started in the spring of 1906, it was still a two-legged [people-centered] operation as it had been from the start. . . . The engines and chassis were produced in the manufacturing workshops, then moved over to be assembled at the Piquette Avenue plant."

THE PLAN

Rather than continue to argue publicly with Malcomson, Ford and Couzens devised a three-stage plan to become independent of Malcomson and the Dodges. First, Ford, Couzens, and Wills gathered statistics on the cost of labor and used them to convince the other stockholders that company profits depended on reducing the number of manpower hours per car.

Second, on November 22, 1905, Ford used his money to start a new company, the Ford Manufacturing Company. Its purpose was to produce engines, running gears, and the other car parts that the Dodge brothers had been making. The new company, owned entirely by Ford, would be so efficient, he said, that it could sell motors, transmissions, and other parts cheaper than the Dodges could, thereby making more profit for the stockholders.

Finally, Ford and Couzens never told the other stockholders that their goal was to put Ford in control of the Ford Motor Company. And no one Malcomson, in particular, seemed to catch on. Even though Malcomson knew that the Ford Manufacturing Company was starting, he did not realize that if Henry Ford's new company took over the Dodges' role in the total production of cars, the Ford Motor Company would be only a fraction of the operation. Since neither the Dodges nor Malcomson had stock in the new Ford Manufacturing Company, the stock they did own would constitute less than half the business.

About a week later, Malcomson realized that with only 25 percent of the stock in the Ford Motor Company and none in the Ford Manufacturing Company, he would lose any decision-making power he had, including the production of the Model K. When he became aware of this, though, it was too late to change things at Ford. Thus, he started another company, hoping to make money on his own. Malcomson's new company would sell another automobile called the Aerocar.

With this action, though, Malcomson made a mistake. The Aerocar was in direct competition with the Ford Motor Company's product. To the other stockholders, such competition from a fellow stockholder was unfair and intended to reduce their profits. They pointed out the conflict of interest and asked him to resign.

Malcomson did resign. He also put his 25 percent of the Ford Motor Company stock up for sale. However, because of Ford Motor Company rules, only other stockholders could buy it. Henry Ford bought Malcomson's stock for $175,000 in July 1906, a 700 percent increase on a $25,000 investment.

On the day he bought out Malcomson's stock, Ford's vision of the future of the au-tomotive industry took shape. Not only would he not make luxury cars such as the Model K, but he would make a car that the average person could afford. This was why he was willing to pay so much money for Malcomson's stock. And rightly so. Ford's company was about to sell ten thousand cars in a single year. Driving home with Ford Company mechanic Fred Rockelman after that historic stock purchase, Ford said, "Fred, this is a great day. We're going to expand this company, and you will see that it will grow by leaps and bounds. The proper system, as I have it in mind, is to get the car to the multitude."[39]

TAKING CONTROL OF THE FORD MOTOR COMPANY

When Malcomson sold his stock in the Ford Motor Company, four other stockholders also decided to sell. After all the buying and selling, Ford owned 585 of the 1,000 shares. Owning a majority of the stock gave Ford the control he had wanted. According to Lacey, "In the final analysis, Henry Ford had no need of—these men [the stockholders who remained], and henceforward, his control over the Ford Motor Company would be absolute."[40]

Without delay, Couzens nominated Ford to be president of the company. He was elected at the next board meeting. Soon after that election, the board approved the new president's plan to join the Ford Manufacturing Company with the Ford Motor Company, making the Ford Manufacturing Company nonexistent. The new company was called simply the Ford Motor Company.

The next thing to decide was where the company's new manufacturing plant would be built. The old plants had been getting more and more crowded as orders came in and as more employees were hired to assemble enough cars to meet demands. After some investigating, Ford thought he had found just the right place: a fifty-seven-acre abandoned racetrack northeast of downtown Detroit. The site was a good choice because it had connections to roads and railroads and was large enough to accommodate the growing company.

Once again, Ford's vision prevailed. The board of the Ford Motor Company approved the purchase of the racetrack, located in the Detroit suburb of Highland Park. Then they allowed expenditures of more than $500,000 for the buildings that would be needed at the manufacturing plant.

The Ford family with friends aboard a Model K, the short-lived and expensive luxury car.

A WOULD-BE MONOPOLIST

In 1903 George Baldwin Selden, an unsuccessful designer of gasoline engines and president of the Association of Licensed Automobile Manufacturers, sued Ford for infringing on his U.S. patent gasoline engines. Biographer James Brough in The Ford Dynasty *describes the way Selden developed his attack on the Ford Motor Company.*

"[After] George Baldwin Selden, a gray-bearded patent attorney of Rochester, New York . . . tried and failed repeatedly to construct a successful working engine to call his own, he used his professional knowledge to take him along an easier road. In precise legal language, he described the motor and carriage that had eluded him and, with accompanying diagram, filed it as an application to the United States Patent Office. . . . In Edsel's birthday month [November 1893], the deliberately delayed patent was finally issued in Washington. In Selden's hands, it would serve as a pistol aimed at the head of the infant [automobile] industry to exact a toll in royalties to be paid to him.

[Selden's 1903] lawsuit filed in New York [claimed Ford] was infringing the Selden patent, to which the twenty-six member firms of the association [ALAM] had exclusive right since they paid royalties of 1.25 per cent of the sales price on every vehicle they produced. . . . The association [advertised] its member firms, . . . warning that 'No other manufacturers or importers are authorized to make or sell gasoline automobiles, and any person making, selling or using such machines made or sold by any unlicensed manufacturers or importers will be liable to prosecution.'"

THE RISKS FORD WAS TAKING

In 1906, Ford's vision was revolutionary. He wanted to create a huge company that not only assembled cars but also made the parts, something no one else in industry was doing at the time. However, three factors made the venture look risky.

First, other car manufacturers were still using the traditional approach; that is, they were building expensive cars for wealthy buyers. The Olds Motor Works, for example, was marketing an expensive Oldsmobile. In Europe, Rolls Royce continued to appeal to the wealthier buyers. Only one American company, the Hudson Motor Company, was making a bid to sell cars in the low-to-moderate price range.

A second concern had to do with the American government. President Theodore Roosevelt's administration wanted to reduce the power of businesses called trusts. Trusts were made of one or more firms that combined to reduce competition in the marketplace. These trusts created monopolies that reduced the number of companies from which consumers could choose to buy a given product. In turn, the monopoly company could raise its prices and overcharge American buyers. Combining Ford's assembly and manufacturing companies could be seen as forming a trust, which might make the company a target of the Roosevelt administration's trust-busting policies.

Finally, Ford was resisting rising pressure from the Association of Licensed Automobile Manufacturers (ALAM), an organized group of companies in the car industry. The ALAM was organized in 1899 by patent lawyer George Baldwin Selden. In 1903, Selden, who held one of the earliest U.S. patents on gasoline motors, charged that Ford had used his patent and had no right to manufacture cars without paying royalties to the ALAM.

GETTING THE CAR TO THE MULTITUDE

Convinced that once he had control of his company he could reach the goal he had set, to get the car to the multitude, Ford considered the risks to be merely challenges to be dealt with one at a time. For example, the challenge of deviating from the standard of the time in an effort to sell larger quantities of less expensive cars could, he thought, be met primarily by designing a car that would be worth the price the average person could pay.

Ford met the second challenge, the Roosevelt administration's determination to break the power of trusts, by simply going ahead with his plan to join the Ford Motor Company and the Ford Manufacturing Company. He was confident that his companies had been so well combined into one that they could not be considered a trust.

Ford met the third challenge by insisting that his lawyers win the Selden lawsuit. He believed that his Ford motor was nothing like the patent held by George Selden. He convinced his lawyers to learn more about the way his motor worked and to study Selden's patent thoroughly.

Then, satisfied by how the risks would be overcome, Ford addressed another problem. He had to figure out how to keep down the expense of building cars. This would be the only way he could make a car cheaply enough to attract average buyers.

A STRONG NEW STEEL

Ford's first concerns were design related and he focused primarily on strength and reliability. Knowing that the metal he was using for certain parts, such as the gears, was too brittle, Ford was always on the lookout for a stronger kind of steel. He knew that if the gears broke, the car would be useless and the average buyer would not be able to fix it. He wanted to guarantee that his car would be more rugged than anything else on the market.

One place Ford liked to visit to look for ideas was the racetrack. Here, he knew, the strongest possible materials would be used because race cars had to give the highest possible performance under pressure. At one race, after seeing a race car go out of control, he went out to inspect the wreckage.

The wrecked race car had been manufactured in France. Even though many parts had broken, Ford noticed one small valve strip that seemed to be made of a stronger steel. Immediately interested, he picked it up, had it analyzed, and found that the steel contained the element vanadium.

Importing vanadium steel alloys from France would be prohibitively expensive, though, so Ford researched the possibility of having the steel made in the United States. He found a steel plant in Canton, Ohio, that was willing to remodel its foundry and produce a vanadium alloy. The product the plant sold to Ford had ten times the strength of other steel being made in the United States at the time.

Ford first used vanadium steel in his Model N. Over the first weeks of its production, even more vanadium steel went into its parts. This and the redesign of its carburetor and ignition made the car stronger and faster than previous models. Says biographer Brough, "[The] peppy little runabout [with its] fifteen-horsepower engine would make forty-five miles an hour."[41]

Ford hoped to produce ten thousand Model Ns at an unbelievably low cost of $450 a piece. These predictions were a little off, though. The Ford Motor Company did make more than ten thousand Model Ns in 1907, but they sold for $650 each. Regardless of the miscalculation, sales went so well that the Ford Motor Company made a $1 million profit from the Model N. And since more than half of the Company's stocks belonged to Ford, more than half of that profit belonged to him.

THE DESIGNER'S STUDIO

The profits Ford made from the sales of the Model N proved what Ford had been saying all along, that it was good for business to cater to the average buyer. His next step would be a car that was even lighter, stronger, and faster than the Model N. This car would sell cheaply enough that even more of the general public could buy it.

With the new plant at Highland Park still in the planning stages, Ford ordered a special designing room to be built on the top floor of the existing Ford Motor Company plant, located on Detroit's Piquette Avenue. In this room, just big enough to hold a blackboard, several machines and power tools, Ford's mother's old rocking chair, and a working model, Ford began designing another new car that he hoped would surprise competing carmakers and dominate the market.

His work was top secret, and he chose only a few key people to join him behind the room's locked doors. These men included engineer C. Harold Wills; woodcrafter Charles Sorensen, who would carve wooden models of parts; draftsman Joseph Galamb; and Spider Huff, who had a background in electricity.

There were other helpers, too, although these men were not as close to the actual design. Instead, they were a kind of spy corps, finding out what was being done elsewhere. Specifically, they were hired to search out special new kinds of steel and bring in for study cars being made by other manufacturers.

Spectators examine the wreckage of a French race car. Henry Ford frequented the racetrack, examining wrecked race cars in search of ideas to improve his own automobile designs.

"I WONDER IF WE CAN DO IT"

Ford and his men worked long hours for more than a year. Once the new car's motor was designed, all of its parts were made half-scale, put together, and tested. Many of these models were built only to be torn down, remade, and reassembled. Ford used his leadership skills to keep his men working hard. And work they did, as Ford stood nearby coaxing, saying, "I wonder if we can do it. I wonder."[42]

The new design was Ford's, but he did not do it alone. He utilized the experience and education of his workers—the electrician, draftsman, woodcrafter, and his spies. He tested and studied all the ideas and models they brought in. As Allan Nevins explains,

> [Ford] would bring into the room a proposal, usually his own, but sometimes owing much to a rival machine or an associate, and [draftsman Joseph]

THE SOCIOLOGICAL DEPARTMENT

Although he did not generally support charities, Henry Ford did believe that helping people be able to support themselves was a worthwhile cause. In his book Henry Ford: An Interpretation, *Reverend Samuel S. Marquis, who worked for Ford from 1915 until 1921, quotes Ford's reasons for starting the Sociological Department, an organization aimed at teaching heads of families how to economize and lead moral lives.*

"We are planning to help the man who is weak and needs our help. We are going to go along with him in a friendly way until he is able to walk alone. And more than that, I believe that the great majority of men may be trusted to do the right thing if given the chance. There are thousands of men out there in the shop who are not living as they should. Their homes are crowded and insanitary. Wives are going out to work because their husbands are unable to earn enough to support the family. They fill up their homes with roomers and boarders in order to help swell the income. It's all wrong—all wrong. It's especially bad for the children. They are neglected from necessity. Now, these people are not living in this manner as a matter of choice. Give them a decent income and they will live decently—will be glad to do so. What they need is the opportunity to do better, and some one to take a little personal interest in them—some one who will show that he has faith in them."

Galamb would turn it into both blueprints and graphic sketches. Sometimes Ford, scanning the diagrams, would seize a pencil and draw a rough, amateurish sketch himself. . . . When blueprints were ready, parts were cast, machined, and put together. . . . Like other engineers of that period, Ford liked to construct a working model to "see why it doesn't work."[43]

The men worked on many parts. They constructed a new carburetor. They also improved the starter and the springs. Thanks to those efforts, they had workable results by March 1908. Their plans for the car, as Nevins writes, defined the "fundamental character" of what was "really a revolutionary product."[44]

Six months ahead of the planned October 1908 release date, the Ford Motor Company sent out its first advertisements for its newest car, the Model T. At $825, its price was just slightly under the price of the new Buick. Ford was on the verge of making millions.

4 The Millionaire

Both the Model T and its production methods were unprecedented in the field of transportation. And the car was well received.

Before it went on the market, however, some people wondered how successful it would be. Initially, even Ford himself wondered if the company would manage to sell ten thousand cars. And people who watched the construction of the Highland Park manufacturing plant wondered when Ford would go broke from the expense. But they need not have been concerned. The Model T was destined to bring its designer more wealth and its company more fame than any other single car.

MODEL T INNOVATIONS

The reason the Model T was so well received was that it was stronger, much more maneuverable, and faster than any competitor's car. To achieve this, the new car combined a unique motor design with a lightweight frame and many important new features.

Among those features were several aimed at attracting average buyers. To keep the Model T from breaking down frequently and being a repair nuisance to its owner, for example, the Ford team built many of the car's parts out of vanadium

A father and daughter with their Model T. The Model T's lightweight frame and high floorboard appealed to average citizens.

steel. This innovation kept the transmission going and the car running even under intense pressure. And to make the car easy to maneuver, Ford installed a high floorboard that cleared ruts in the road, a two-pedal control (one pedal for forward gear, the other for reverse), and a steering wheel that was easy to turn. Such ease was important since most Model T buyers would be used to driving a horse and buggy; just a simple slap of the reins and a word to the horses made that vehicle move.

Certainly, all of these innovations were a result of the hard work of Ford's team. But,

says Nevins, "when all allowances were made, we must repeat that general credit for the Model T unquestionably goes to Henry Ford. His was the controlling plan for a light, powerful, trustworthy cheap car; his was the guiding mind; his was clearly the most powerful personality."[45]

THE HIGHLAND PLANT

From March to October 1908, dealers cleared their salesrooms to make room for the Model T. They sent in their orders by tele-

Assembly workers lower the body of a Model T onto a chassis at the Highland Park plant.

graph, telephone, and mail, and the plant on Piquette Avenue went into double shifts. Once the initial orders were filled, they were followed by an avalanche of new orders, and the Piquette Avenue plant could not keep up.

So, Ford's team concentrated on making the manufacturing process practical. When the new Highland Park factory opened, they wanted every machine to make every part accurately. Furthermore, parts would be interchangeable and there would be enough of them on hand to keep the assembly lines busy at all times.

The Model T assembly building that took shape at Highland Park was three stories high and full of windows. The building's natural lighting made it easier for the workers to see what they were doing and also saved on electricity. In front of the building there was a huge open field where finished automobiles could be lined up for transportation to destinations all over the country.

Construction was completed during the first months of 1910, and the Ford Motor Company quickly moved Model T production to Highland Park. The design of the production facilities proved efficient. After the move, all previous sales and production records were beaten. In 1910, 18,664 Model Ts were made and sold, and production doubled the following year. Profits soared so high that the $500,000 spent to build the Highland Park factory seemed minimal. Consequently, in 1911 the Ford Motor Company earned $1 million in dividends. Nearly 60 percent of the earnings belonged to Henry Ford himself.

CHALLENGE FROM A MONOPOLIST

About this time, one of the risks the Ford Motor Company had been taking resurfaced. With the release of the Model T and news of its immense profits, the ALAM, which by 1910 included 90 percent of Ford's competitors, began a nationwide advertising campaign. In its ads, it charged Ford with denying the association its rightful royalties (for use of Selden's patent) and claimed that Ford owed millions of dollars in back payments. The ALAM and George Selden won an initial patent lawsuit in 1909, but Ford appealed the decision to the U.S. Circuit Court of Appeals.

The war of words did not stop there. Selden followed up his win by advertising that anyone who bought a Ford car would also be responsible for paying back royalties. Ford retaliated by assuring his customers that he would personally cover any court-ordered payment leveled against a Model T owner.

Ford's appeal went to court in late 1910. Ford's lawyers, having studied Selden's patent, argued that the design had added nothing to Ford's cars. Ultimately, Ford's lawyers demonstrated that none of the Ford motors were like the Selden motor and that, in fact, the Selden motor did not work. This time, the trial ended differently. The court ruled on January 9, 1911, that Ford owed no royalties.

Winning this highly publicized lawsuit bolstered Ford's sales. Average people who had never thought of buying a car now sympathized with Ford. They were encouraged by Ford's guarantee of performance and his offer to make good if any

HIGHLAND PARK PLANT PRODUCES THE MODEL T

In Henry Ford: His Life, His Work, His Genius, *biographer William Adams Simonds describes the success of Model T production at Ford's Highland Park facility.*

"Commencement of production in the Highland Park Plant marked the beginning of the swift upsurge of Ford cars, and at the same time the first use of what is called 'mass production' in the automobile industry. . . . The figures mounted skyward: 10,607 cars in 1909; 18,664 cars in 1910, first year of the new plant; 34,528 cars in 1911. These big gains were almost infinitesimal compared with those that followed: 1912, 78,440 cars; 1913, 168,220 cars; 1914, 248,307 cars.

The annual cash receipts jumped from a little over $9,000,000 to nearly $120,000,000 in the same period. Profits went from $3,125,875.58 in 1909 to approximately $25,000,000 in 1914."

court order were leveled against a Model T purchaser. Ford's profits continued to rise as sales increased.

IMPROVING EFFICIENCY EVEN MORE

The favorable ruling in the Selden lawsuit brought in so many orders for Model Ts that even the Highland Park plant's production capabilities were strained. To keep dealers from having to wait, Ford began to study how to make production even more efficient.

To accomplish this goal, he hired an adviser named Frederick Taylor to analyze the company's assembly process and suggest ways that it could be improved. Taylor noticed immediately that the process had changed little since the formation of the Ford Motor Company, even though workers were now putting together thousands

more cars. After doing several studies, Taylor suggested some changes.

To begin with, he thought it would be a good idea for Ford workers to specialize. Rather than have the same men put together an entire car, Taylor thought each one should become an expert in one or two parts. Then, each man or group would assemble the part he knew best and send the unfinished car on to the next group, who would do the same. In this way, the workers would save time by not having to switch tasks during the day; instead, they could concentrate on doing one job as quickly as possible.

Next, Taylor suggested that Ford workers eliminate all excess movement between tasks. In particular, having workers hand-deliver parts from one station to the next, Taylor said, wasted a lot of time. To solve this problem, Ford decided to redesign the factory so that gravity did that extra work. Biographer Keith Sward writes,

The company finally eliminated . . . waste motion by making an original application of an old ideal. It installed a continuous series of gravity-slides, leading from one bench to the next. Now the moment a worker finished his particular operation, he could turn to an inclined trough at his elbow and let go of the piece he had been working on; it slid down the incline and arrived at the next work-place automatically. This innovation, introduced [in the Highland plant] in 1910, brought a new tempo to the production line; it sped up particularly the processing of parts that were small and light.[46]

The Ford technicians applied the changes to each department, and in 1911 and 1912 the speed of the assembly lines doubled. Yet, by 1913, production was again barely able to keep up with the orders received by the sales department.

THE BIG FIVE-O

The year 1913 was a good one for Henry Ford. He celebrated his fiftieth birthday on July 30. His son, Edsel, graduated from high school and began working for the Ford Motor Company. And important new strides were made in improving assembly-line production. In that year, Lacey writes,

Ford was scaling extraordinary new peaks of power, wealth and creativity. Far from losing momentum, he was intensifying his capacity to do several things at once. Through the summer months of 1913, he was working on

the details of belts, chutes, and slides which were to revolutionize the twentieth century workplace.[47]

By Ford's fiftieth birthday, with orders for cars twice that of the previous year, workers at Highland Park could make a Model T in twelve hours and twenty-eight minutes. Despite this, the plant was still barely keeping up with orders. Ford was convinced that sales would more than double the next year and the year after, with no foreseeable letdown. Thus, he insisted that even faster production was necessary.

Auto workers assemble Model T frames. By 1913 workers could build a Model T in less than twelve and a half hours.

THE MOVING ASSEMBLY LINE

Ford's next assembly innovation changed the face of manufacturing. According to Sward, it "set the mold for all future developments in automotive technology."[48]

On January 14, 1914, Ford and a team of efficiency experts introduced the motorized, or moving, assembly line. The moving assembly line used a series of motorized conveyor belts and pulleys to move cars from one stage of production to another. The workers simply added their parts as the car went by. By introducing this new feature, the Ford Motor Company reduced the time it took to assemble a Model T by 50 percent.

This increase in efficient assembly called for increased efficiency in parts manufacturing. Thus, Ford installed new, fast machines to drill holes and bend, shape, grind, stamp, or cut the metal for each part. If a machine broke down or worked too slowly, Ford, unwilling to waste time, simply replaced it. Says biographer James Brough,

> The great majority of parts were made on the premises. Machines shaped crankcases from sheets of steel, curled gas-tank heads, and drilled forty-five holes in a cylinder block at a time. Presses produced a radiator's ninety-five tubes in one stroke. Any one of the fifteen thousand items of contributory machinery that churned out axles, wheels, brake bands, gears, and the rest would be scrapped after as little as a month's use if the design departments could devise something better, something to shave an extra fraction

from time spent in assembly. No other manufacturer sold enough cars to afford to follow suit.[49]

THE $5 DAY

One of the reasons the motorized assembly line worked so well was that Ford also raised the salaries of his workers, a decision he made just before installing the motorized assembly line. Since Ford had wrested control of the company from Malcomson, profits had risen dramatically; increased Model T sales had only boosted them more. Yet the workers' pay—$2.50 a day, the standard of the time—had not changed.

At a board meeting on January 5, 1914, Ford and the other stockholders discussed this issue. It was only good business, Ford said, to increase the workers' salaries. Ford hoped that increasing salaries would make employees work harder to produce more cars. His suggestion was successful. By the end of the meeting, the stockholders voted to double the workers' pay to $5.00 a day.

The announcement of the $5 day appeared in newspapers all over the United States and quickly caused some problems. Biographer Roger Burlingame explains:

> The sudden news brought ten thousand job-hunters from all over the country to the Highland Park gates. A Detroit winter is not a comfortable setting for such a gathering. The week of the announcement was a peculiarly bitter [cold] one. When word reached the huge crowd that, naturally, there were not jobs for ten thousand new-

WORKER BURNOUT

Although the institution of the $5 day brought many hopeful workers to the Ford Motor Company, some burned out quickly, a result of a stressful work environment. One employee, Charles A. Madison, left Ford at the beginning of 1914 after only one week because he found the demands there to be too rigorous and exhausting. Madison's story is told in Robert Lacey's book Ford: The Men and the Machine.

"After only a week at Highland Park, [Madison] returned to [competing car manufacturer] Dodge. He had not realised he would have to work six months before qualifying for his profit-sharing bonus, and even at $5.00 a day he decided he could never work at Ford. He had intellectual taste and had felt 'too fatigued after leaving the Ford factory to do any serious reading or attend a play or concert.'

Madison settled for $3.00 a day, the more relaxed and friendly atmosphere of the Dodge plant, and the energy and appetite for some life of his own after he had clocked out from work. His brief week at Ford remained in his mind 'a rancorous memory—a form of hell on earth that turned human beings into driven robots.' . . .

Madison had found himself shadowed by stopwatch wielders and harassed by his foreman, who seemed harassed in turn by his own superiors. The only way Madison could keep up with his production schedule, he discovered, was to work right through his eight-hour shift without a break, munching on a sandwich while endeavouring to keep pace with his machine."

comers, a riot started. There is no doubt that the company should have made provision for this result and for the orderly handling of applicants, but apparently no one had thought of that, expecting only sweetness and light to surround the generous gesture. The ultimate tragedy came when, at their wits' end, the local police turned freezing water from a fire hose upon the unhappy crowd. [50]

For Ford, however, results were mainly positive. Following the introduction of the $5 day, production picked up even more speed, and sales improved. According to the *Literary Digest*,

> Six weeks after the [$5 day] plan went into effect in his factory a comparison was made between the production for January, 1914, and January, 1913. In 1913, with 16,000 men working on the actual production of cars for ten hours a day, 16,000 cars were made and shipped. Under the new plan, 15,800 men working eight hours a day made and shipped 26,000 cars. [51]

Following the $5 day plan, production of the Model T improved significantly.

NEW TYPES OF WORKERS

In addition to instituting the $5 day, Ford also liberalized his hiring practices. Ford hired more women than other companies and paid them better. He also hired some workers who had handicaps; being confined to a wheelchair, Ford said, did not reduce a person's capability. He hired ex-convicts with the aim of redeeming them from a life of crime, and in 1914 Ford hired William Perry, the company's first black worker.

Another workforce change involved introducing a new position. In 1909, Ford hired one of the company's first secretaries. She was sixteen-year-old Evangeline Coté. "Evangeline," writes Lacey, "was a woman who had the ability to get things done. She was not afraid to make decisions on her own initiative and this won her the especial favor of Ford, who liked to delegate problems to subordinates and then forget about them."[52]

Adding new workers, both on the assembly line and in the offices, meant that it was harder for Ford to keep up his practice of being fully aware of what all workers were expected to do. As the number of secretaries at the company grew, Ford's contacts with these women often took the place of worker contacts on the assembly line. And Evangeline Coté became Ford's trusted confidante.

THE FORD HOSPITAL

In 1914, Ford became a millionaire. He also agreed to participate in a philanthropic project in Detroit, even though he generally disliked charity. He served as the fundraising chairman for the development of a new hospital.

Ford failed, however, as a fund-raiser. He did not like to ask people for money. It was not charity but hard work, he said, that was good for people. As a result, he raised no money, and hospital construction came to a stop.

Ford still believed that the hospital was necessary, though. Detroit's population had grown so rapidly that the city's old hospital was overcrowded. So, Ford resigned as fund-raising chairman and took on all the project's debts. Construction resumed, and the hospital, called the Ford Hospital, was ready to open in 1917.

THE PLAN OF THE FORD HOSPITAL

In his memoir Today and Tomorrow, *Henry Ford describes the type of doctor employed by the Ford Hospital and explains the living conditions of nurses studying at the Henry Ford Hospital School of Nursing and Hygiene. The credentials of the doctors and the satisfaction of the nurses, Ford believed, led to quality health care for patients.*

"This is the plan. The hospital staff, which consists of about one hundred surgeons and physicians, are all on salary from the hospital and do not engage in private practice. There are six services—Medicine, Surgery, Obstetrics, Pediatrics, Laboratory, and X-Ray. Each of these services is headed by men of recognized attainments. In the beginning, there was a preponderance of Johns Hopkins [University, a prominent medical school] men, but as the hospital has grown the staff has ceased to be representative of any single school. Now the men are so drawn that some fifteen or twenty of the leading medical schools in this country and Canada are represented. . . .

Last year, we made provision for pupil nurses by opening the Clara Ford Nurses' Home [dormitory] and the Henry Ford Hospital School of Nursing and Hygiene. The underlying thought is to train nurses to a real profession in which the care of the ill will be the sole objective. To this end, the new home has considerably better appointments than the most first-class hotels. The home and the educational building are on the hospital grounds but at some distance from the hospital. The home has 309 individual rooms, all finished and furnished alike. Each room has a private bath. The rooms are grouped about central entrances or elevators with a sitting room and kitchenette for each group, to carry out the home idea. Connecting with a reception hall on the first floor are eight small parlours where the young women may entertain friends. Dining rooms, kitchens, laundry, sewing room, and trunk room are in the basement. At the rear of the building is a sunken garden extending out from between the two wings. The whole environment of the dormitory is planned with the aim of providing a complete change of atmosphere for the nurses after leaving the hospital wards or classroom."

The Ford Hospital ultimately became a leading teaching and research institution in the Midwest. There were three reasons for this. First, it opened just as the United States entered World War I. Immediately, it began to serve casualties from the war, something that exposed doctors to many wounds and traumas not usually brought to U.S. treatment centers, thus expanding their medical experience. Second, after the war, when the Ford Hospital opened as a private health care facility, it became the first hospital in the United States to admit and treat psychiatric patients.

The third reason for the hospital's prominence in the field of medicine was that Ford himself directed its policy. And Henry Ford believed that hospital care, even the human body, was like a Model T assembly line. "It is my shop," Ford said, "where I hope people can get well as rapidly as possible and have their injured parts repaired."[53] Thus, doctors were encouraged to study a sick person's system. This approach, called systematic diagnosis, involved studying a patient's body parts and functions (blood pressure, heartbeat, urine samples, etc.). Such study laid the foundation for the hospital's research background and led to later development, including the heart-lung machine and open-heart surgery.

THE *PEACE SHIP*

While Ford was building the Ford Hospital, he was aware of armed conflict in southern Europe. A Serbian assassin had killed Archduke Franz Ferdinand of Austria-Hungary on June 28, 1914. By August of that year, all of Europe was at war.

Ford himself was, at least initially, against the war in Europe. He considered himself a pacifist and was against war of any kind. Burlingame writes,

> From the outbreak, in Europe, of the First World War [in August 1914], Ford had grown increasingly pacifist. His particular kind of success had depended on a free economy impossible in wartime. [It] was unbearable to him that . . . [economic] progress should be interrupted. He [also] had . . . a very genuine hatred of killing in any form and . . . the normal performance of an army was, to him, just plain murder.[54]

As World War I continued, Ford became involved with an independent group of international pacifists led by Hungarian activist Rosika Schwimmer. Schwimmer and her followers needed money to finance a peace mission. And so, says Burlingame, "they looked for a millionaire to finance a publicity campaign for the project."[55]

Ford was a good candidate. He first met with Schwimmer on November 22, 1915, and discussed her idea that private citizens from a neutral country, like the United States, could form a peace delegation of mediators. The mediators, then, could hopefully end the conflict. Pleased with Schwimmer's idea, Ford provided the money for her project. A ship, the *Oscar II*, was chartered and renamed the *Peace Ship*. It was scheduled to leave New York on December 4, 1915, with a full load of U.S. peace volunteers.

Pacifism, however, was not popular in the United States at the time. After German submarines sank the U.S. ship the *Lusitania*

The Peace Ship *arrives in New York in 1916.*

in May 1915, many Americans favored entering the war. Such sentiment undermined the *Peace Ship*'s mission. In addition, President Woodrow Wilson did not endorse the mission, although he sympathized with its aims. As a result, the peace mission ultimately failed, and on April 6, 1917, the United States entered the war.

THE SUM TOTAL

It is almost impossible to overestimate Ford's importance by the beginning of World War I. Not only had his manufactur-

ing methods become standard in industry, but Ford himself had become a well-known figure. People listened to him on many topics, from higher wages for workers, to health care, to mass production, to peace. Sward summarizes Ford's achievement:

> On the threshold [beginning] of his fabulous career, Ford hardly looked the part of the empire-builder. In appearance and manner alone, he was anything but the "born" leader. He was shy; he had the rustic mien [look of a farmer]. Nor was youth or education on his side. . . . Of books and formal

A Hard Man to Photograph

In his book of essays Henry Ford: An Interpretation, *Reverend Samuel S. Marquis discusses the difficulty of capturing Ford's face in a photograph or painting.*

"Photographers complain that he [Ford] is 'hard to get.' There are snapshots of him a-plenty. Each looks as he looks at times. No satisfactory photograph of him, so far as I know, has ever been taken. No life-like portrait of him has ever been painted, that I have seen, and I venture to say none revealing the inward man ever will be. There is something in his face too elusive either for camera or brush, just as there is something deep within him so complex, so contradictory, so elusive as to defy description. It is a face that reveals an extraordinary alertness rather than depth of thought. Poise and repose are not present to any marked degree.

The face of Henry Ford is the mirror of his mind. One is as difficult to photograph as the other. Mental snapshots there are of him in abundance, but anything approaching a true mental portrait [personality analysis] of him has never yet been made. Henry Ford to be known must be seen in action, not once or twice, but many times. The only mental picture of him possible is a moving mental picture, a series of impressions, of sketches made on the spot, revealing him swayed, as he is, by various and conflicting thoughts and emotions."

education, even in his special sphere, he knew next to nothing. His, for better or for worse, was the equipment of the shrewd, ingenious, persevering Yankee mechanic. . . . As his company gradually took on stature, Ford proceeded to measure up on many counts to the great work that opened before him. He had a remarkable knack at judging men and performance at the bench, and he made the most of it. . . . The end-effect was outstanding.[56]

5 Conflict and Control

The money and fame that came with Ford's success were certainly welcomed and afforded him luxuries he had never known. In 1915, Ford used a significant portion of his wealth to build himself and his family a large new home. He hired well-known architect Frank Lloyd Wright to design the house. Called Fair Lane and built near Clara Ford's childhood home in Dearborn, the new home was a marvel. It contained numerous bedroom suites, large living rooms, and ornate fireplaces. The grounds surrounding the house were just as lavish and included a pony barn, a man-made lake, and several gardens.

Yet Ford's success also brought problems. The company's prosperity only fueled his desire to acquire complete control of the Ford Motor Company. This desire, and the conflict that resulted from it, determined Ford's decision making in the years during and just after World War I.

THE ROUGE RIVER PROPERTY

The U.S. entry into World War I quickly began to affect Henry Ford. When he realized that German submarine attacks on American ships affected his overseas sales, he rethought his pacifist stance and offered to put his company behind the war effort. First, he contracted to make tractors for Britain. Then he agreed to cooperate with the U.S. Navy, building submarine chasers.

The Ford Motor Company was well prepared to help in these two areas. The company already owned a suitable piece of land, separate from the Highland Park plant, where the tractor and navy ventures could be built. In 1916, Ford had spent his own money to buy several hundred acres of property. Realizing that the company had no room to expand around the Highland Park property, which was crowded and enclosed by other development, he had searched for and found a good place to enlarge his production facilities.

The property was in Dearborn, where Ford grew up. Located on the Rouge River, which emptied into Lake Erie, the site was open to ocean traffic. Even more important, railroad lines passed through the Rouge River acreage, providing access to an important source of raw materials, the iron mines of northern Michigan.

THE WAR EFFORT

Thanks to the Rouge River property, Ford made two significant contributions to the war effort. The new tractor plant, called the Fordson Company, went up first on the Rouge property. Fordson produced thousands of tractors that advanced Britain's agricultural development and sustained the country during World War I.

The second contribution, the navy venture, began operating on May 7, 1918. This was also successful. The navy hired Ford to make 112 submarine chasers, called Eagle boats. Eight weeks later, the first Eagle boat was launched. But because of several abrupt changes in the navy's design specifications, submarine chaser production did not meet expectations. Nevertheless, the navy launched a total of eight Eagle boats in the six months before the end of the war.

RUNNING FOR SENATOR

Immediately following the end of World War I in the fall of 1918, President Woodrow Wilson called on Ford to resume his pacifist stance. Wilson wanted Ford to help him promote world peace through the es-

Edsel Ford operates a Fordson tractor. Fordson tractor production helped advance Britain's agricultural production during World War I.

THE DIE-HARD PACIFIST

For much of his life, Henry Ford remained a pacifist who spoke out against the practice of war. He also believed, though, that many pacifists did not address the real cause of war. In My Philosophy of Industry, *he wrote the following.*

"What causes war is not patriotism, not that human beings are willing to die in defense of their dearest ones. It [the cause of war] is the false doctrine, fostered by the few, that war spells gain. It is this that makes war, and there are not enough pacifists who see it and attack it. The fact that pacifists are left in peace is proof they are not attacking the real causes of war. If pacifists spoke the truth, they would not be petted as they are to-day; theirs would be the hard lot of the martyrs of Truth."

tablishment of the League of Nations, the predecessor of the United Nations. Knowing that at least one more vote was needed in the U.S. Senate to ratify the League of Nations treaty, Wilson asked Ford to run for the office of U.S. senator from Michigan.

Thus, Ford entered the political arena. Much respected by the general population, he won the primary election over the other Democratic candidate, William Alden Smith, by four thousand votes.

Victory should have been easy in the general election. Ford's opponent was Republican Truman H. Newberry, who was against the $5 workday. Ford, however, made almost no effort to campaign on his own behalf. He made no public speeches, issued no public statements, and refused to spend any money on ads. He did this because he believed that news articles were sufficient publicity and that his name and reputation would carry him into the Senate seat.

The strategy did not work. Ford lost the 1918 election, but by only 7,567 votes. Fur-

thermore, the United States never became part of the League of Nations.

FORD'S NEWSPAPER

After losing the Senate race, Ford purchased his hometown newspaper, the *Dearborn Independent,* in November 1918. Its first issue under Ford's ownership was published on January 11, 1919. The newspaper's purpose, as stated on its editorial page, was to publish firsthand news about the Ford Motor Company.

In actuality, Ford used the *Dearborn Independent* to present his own personal opinions. In the hands of its editor, William J. Cameron, the newspaper advocated such things as the nationalization of telegraphs and railroads, better housing for the average citizen, the League of Nations plan, criminalization of alcohol consumption, and women's rights. In these areas, Ford showed his desire to help ordinary people and to make a better world.

COUNTRY ENTERTAINMENT

During the years 1920 to 1922, Henry Ford used his newspaper, the Dearborn Independent, *to promote his ideas. One of his prejudices, anti-Semitism, showed up frequently. Sometimes it was blatant. Other times, it was subtle, as in this excerpt from the article "Jewish Jazz Becomes Our National Music," in which Ford accuses Jews of replacing American classics with mass-produced obscenities. The article is reprinted in* The International Jew.

"The 'popular' song, before it became a Jewish industry, was really popular. The people sang it and had no reason to conceal it. The popular song today is often so questionable a composition that performers with a vestige of decency must appraise their audience before they sing. Citizens of adult age will remember the stages through which the popular song has passed during recent decades. War songs persisted after the Civil War and were gradually intermingled with songs of a later time, picturesque, romantic, clean. The same and similar songs and ballads had a brief revival during World War I. These were not the product of song-factories, but the creation of individuals whose gifts were given natural expression. These individuals did not work for combines of publishers but for the satisfaction of their work, for individual artists of the music-hall stage. There were no great fortunes made out of songs, but there were many satisfactions in having pleased the public taste. . . .

In other days the people sang as they do now, but not in such doped fashion or with such bewildered continuity. They sang because they wished to, not as an uncontrolled habit. They sang songs nonsensical, sentimental, heroic, but the 'shady' songs were outlawed. The old songs come readily back to memory. Though years have intervened since they were the fashion, yet their quality was such that they do not die. The popular song of last month—who knows its name? But there are songs of long ago whose titles are familiar even to those who have not sung them."

However, the paper also turned out to be bitterly anti-Jewish. In the *Dearborn Independent*, Ford and Cameron published more than a hundred anti-Semitic articles. These articles accused the Jews of masterminding every possible problem in society, from corruption in finance to profanity in music to immorality. In an interview with reporter Judson F. Welliver, Ford said,

It is said we are conducting a propaganda against the Jews. We are in fact only trying to awaken the Gentile world to an understanding of what is going on. . . . Our money and banking system is the invention of the Jews for their own purposes of control, and it's bad. Our gold standard was founded by the Jews; it's bad, and things will never get right until we are rid of the power they hold through it.[57]

The DT&I Railroad

Following the purchase of the *Dearborn Independent*, Ford decided to expand his transportation capabilities. In 1922, an opportunity to buy the Detroit, Toledo, and Ironton (DT&I) railroad arose, and Ford took it.

The railroad was hurting financially when Ford got involved. Neighboring navy shipyards needed a deeper harbor at the mouth of the Rouge River and Lake Erie. Plans to enlarge the existing harbor necessitated asking DT&I to destroy its existing bridge across the Rouge River and build a new one, an outlay of $500,000. The railroad's owner's could not afford this, so they asked Ford to finance the bridge by buying bonds. Instead, he offered to buy the railroad. Owning the railroad appealed to Ford for two reasons. First, the DT&I railroad lines came directly to Detroit from coal and iron mines farther south. In addition, the DT&I intersected with fifteen other big railroads. Both advantages would prove beneficial to Ford's company. According to reporter Judson F. Welliver,

> That [rail]road was just what Henry Ford needed. It runs from Detroit south and southeast across Ohio to where Ohio, Kentucky and West Virginia come together. It touches the West Virginia coal regions, and . . . crosses fifteen important railroads—all the big systems. To Ford, it would be invaluable as a terminal facility [a loading and unloading point for transfer to boats, other railroads, and factories]. It would take solid train loads out of his factories to the connecting roads and would insure a steady supply of coal.[58]

Ford turned around the failing DT&I railroad and made it financially successful.

The DT&I Railroad (top) ran right by Ford's plant. The railroad made it easy for Ford to import raw materials.

Using the same business sense that he had in his manufacturing and assembling plants, Ford economized on transportation. Realizing that it wasted space to pack a freight car with assembled automobiles, for example, Ford built assembly plants in other cities. Then he shipped only manufactured parts; cars were assembled in the cities where they would be sold. Furthermore, railroad cars were packed economically, utilizing every bit of space. By eliminating empty space on railroad cars, Ford reduced the number of freight cars needed to carry goods. This ultimately saved money for the railroad. As Ford's friend Garet Garrett writes,

> The first time he made as many as one thousand [Model Ts] in a day and tried to ship them he created the worst [railroad] traffic jam Detroit had ever seen. . . . So he began to ship [the Model Ts] knocked down, to be assembled at the branch plants; and that way he could get one hundred and thirty in one freight car. He went much further. More and more the branch plants all over the country assembled the cars and did also some manufacturing, so that only the subassemblies and the bits and pieces went out from Detroit, and these packed and crated with such geometric precision that a loaded freight car was as full as an eggshell.[59]

TROUBLE FOR THE STOCKHOLDERS

Despite Ford's many successes, he wanted more. He was tired of arguing with and hav-ing to answer to the other stockholders. Ford wanted complete control of his company.

The biggest disagreement between Ford and his fellow stockholders concerned the reinvestment of company profits. Ford had no interest in becoming richer and richer and then borrowing money at interest to enlarge the plant or improve its operation. "There is nothing in saving money," he said. "The thing to do with it is to put it back into yourself, into your work, into the thing that is important, into whatever you are so much interested in that it is more important to you than the money."[60]

The other investors thought differently, however. Two stockholders in particular, John and Horace Dodge, wanted the company's profits divided before reinvestment funds were taken out. The Dodges knew that Ford had produced nearly 45 percent of all automobiles made in the United States during 1915. As a result, their share of the profits should be growing each year. It was not. Thus, they became increasingly determined to get the money they thought Ford owed them. So, when Ford authorized more than $5 million to enlarge the Model T plant and spent another $16.5 million for other projects without consulting the stockholders, John and Horace Dodge sued him.

THE DODGE LAWSUIT

The Dodges' lawsuit got under way in 1917. It dragged on in the court system for more than a year, allowing Henry Ford ample time to think up a way to rid himself and his company of the Dodges' influence.

Edsel and Eleanor Ford. Edsel was elected president of the Ford Motor Company in 1918, after his father's resignation.

On December 30, 1918, Ford resigned as president of the Ford Motor Company. The other stockholders accepted his resignation and elected his son, Edsel, as the company's new president.

A few months later, the Dodge brothers won their lawsuit. On February 7, 1919, Michigan Superior Court judge Russell C. Ostrander ruled that the Ford Motor Company owed John and Horace Dodge more than $20 million. The judge also said the Dodges had the right to participate in making company decisions, including how profits were spent.

Ford, however, was undeterred by the verdict. In March 1919, a Los Angeles newspaper reported that he was organizing a new company, one that he could control completely. His new company's goal, Ford said, was to build a car that was even

The Chicago Tribune *Tower. Henry Ford sued the newspaper for libel in 1919.*

and build a car to compete with the Model T, the Ford Motor Company was certain to lose money. Furthermore, without the support and expertise of Henry Ford, the stockholders feared that Americans would lose confidence in Ford Motor Company cars. When sales dropped and profits fell as a result, the stock the men held would be almost worthless. Hoping to make some money before stock prices plummeted, the stockholders decided to sell.

By July 11, 1919, all the Ford Motor Company's stockholders, including John and Horace Dodge, had sold out. Henry Ford bought their stock. To do this, Ford spent a huge sum of money, more than $100 million. But, to him, it was worth it. Finally, he had the control he wanted. He would have to answer to no one but himself.

THE *CHICAGO TRIBUNE* TRIAL

While Ford was busy taking control of the Ford Motor Company, another legal challenge was going on. This was a lawsuit Henry Ford had filed against a newspaper, the *Chicago Tribune*.

Ford was suing the *Tribune* for libel (attacking someone's character unfairly) because it had published a story that included an error in fact. The *Tribune* claimed that Ford would not pay National Guardsmen who worked for hire for their time serving the army. In reality, however, Ford did pay his National Guard employees and made their jobs available to them when they returned from service. Rather than retract the story, though, the *Tribune* chose to defend itself in court.

cheaper and more reliable than the Model T. He claimed to have been forced into the decision by the judge's verdict in the Dodge lawsuit; paying the Dodges, Ford said, deprived his company of ready cash.

As the news of Ford's starting up a new company spread, the other stockholders, including the Dodges, began to get nervous. If Ford did indeed start up a new company

Under advisement from his lawyer Alfred J. Lucking, Ford sued the newspaper for $1 million in damages, charging the *Tribune* with issuing a paragraph of libelous remarks. Although most of the attacks in the paragraph were false, one, calling Ford "ignorant," was true. Unfortunately, Ford's lawyers did not attempt to omit this word from the lawsuit.

During the trial, which lasted fourteen weeks, Ford's responses during questioning seemed to prove that he was indeed ignorant of many things. The trial's real purpose seemed to get lost as the *Tribune's* attorneys questioned Ford about simple facts, which he often did not know or care about. He failed to answer question after question correctly. He did not know the dates of the American Revolution, the name of the traitor Benedict Arnold, or a host of other dates, definitions, and personalities commonly recognized by most Americans.

When the trial ended, the jury took ten hours to come to a verdict. On August 14, 1919, they declared Ford the winner of the suit. The *Tribune*, the jury said, was guilty of libel. The award they granted, however, was not the $1 million Ford's lawyers had asked for. Instead, the jury gave him only 6 cents.

Ford passed off the tiny award as inconsequential. But he was wounded and he expressed this by blaming the judge, suggesting that the judge had favored the *Tribune*. "Supreme Court judges should be paid as much as the President," Ford said. "Make them so independent that you can get the best men."[61]

TOTAL CONTROL

Following the *Tribune* trial, Ford solidified his control of the Ford Motor Company. Within a year, he divided up the company's

Henry Ford takes the stand during the Chicago Tribune *trial. Although the jury found in favor of Ford, they awarded him only six cents in damages.*

stock among himself (55,212 shares), Edsel (41,652 shares), and Clara (3,136 shares). Then he and his bankers integrated all the smaller companies Ford owned, such as the *Dearborn Independent*, into the larger Ford Motor Company.

All transactions were complete on April 19, 1920. The Ford Motor Company now comprised a massive unit owned entirely by Ford's family. Ford's drive for power, as Allan Nevins and Frank Ernest Hill write, made it certain that "there could now be no challenge to company policy. . . . Ford held in firm hands the tools to implement his many ideas of industrial and social change. He was no longer merely a dreamer; he could act with massive power. He meant to do so. In the new Ford Motor Company he would be complete master."[62]

THE PRESIDENT OF THE FORD MOTOR COMPANY

Henry Ford was complete master of the Ford Motor Company, but he was not the company's president. The president was Ford's twenty-seven-year-old son, Edsel, who had been elected in 1918 when his father resigned.

Edsel Ford's personality contrasted sharply with the rough-and-ready ways of his

Edsel Ford's personality and business approach were markedly different from those of his father.

father. As biographers Nevins and Hill write, Edsel Ford was always "gentlemanly."[63] He was a patient listener and negotiator, courteous, thoughtful, and controlled.

Edsel pleased his father in several ways. He loved designing cars. He paid close attention to detail. He understood company affairs. And when Edsel Ford made a judgment, it was certain to have been well planned and researched.

MANAGEMENT CONFLICTS

It was in his management style, however, that Edsel Ford differed most from Henry Ford. Whereas his father seldom explained himself, Edsel expressed himself with clarity and confidence. Edsel Ford was open and direct. In contrast, Henry Ford had achieved at least some of his control by being unpredictable and secretive (as in the Malcomson and Dodge brothers' conflicts).

Disagreements between Henry Ford and his son became apparent early on. At first, they seemed inconsequential—a matter of sales policy or publicity. Edsel favored advertising, for example, whereas his father was content with headline news, good or bad. As time went on, though, the conflict became much more important.

The main source of conflict stemmed from Edsel's lack of real control over company affairs. Even though Henry Ford had relinquished the presidency, he had not let go of his power. Edsel was company president in name only. If, for example, plant manager Charles Sorensen or company secretary Edward Liebold, both allies of Henry Ford, made a decision the employees did not like (such as firing someone or changing positions on the assembly line), the factory workers would complain to Edsel or to Edsel's friend, personnel manager Ernest Kanzler. Edsel and Kanzler usually listened to these complaints, but there was little they could do. Regardless of their opinion, Sorensen and Liebold, supported by Henry Ford, always had the ultimate say.

Edsel's powerlessness was compounded by his own unwillingness to demand the authority his title afforded him. He usually backed down in the face of scrutiny by his father, Sorensen, or Liebold. And his response to factory workers' pleas that he do something to help them was often a simple, "Well, after all, my father built this business."[64]

Edsel's lack of control and his unwillingness to take it for himself caused two problems: It made the employees lose confidence in his management abilities, and it introduced an element of uneasiness in the workplace. As Henry Ford got older, his personality became even more harsh. This often made the work environment at Ford Motor Company unpleasant. Biographers Nevins and Hill write,

> [Henry] Ford spread uneasiness throughout his vast organization. . . . He would take a keen interest in one man or project, then would drop it completely. He was a creature of moods ("If he saw three blackbirds in

the morning, all birds were black that day"); he cut off explanations with a sudden decision; walked out of a discussion remarking: "I'll be back when you get through talking about this." His officials, all without title, were never sure of their standing. Favored one day, they might be ignored the next. . . . The effect of these unpredictable actions was to produce a tautness in the entire work force, so that a word, a gesture, an act would set it vibrating. [65]

Yet again, it was clear that a change was necessary.

Chapter

6 New Directions

The 1920s brought many changes to the life of Henry Ford. In 1920, the moving assembly line at the Rouge River plant made it possible to turn out a Model T every three minutes, and the outdated Highland Park plant was closed. By July 30, 1923, his sixtieth birthday, Ford had three grandchildren (a fourth was born in 1925). And as the decade wore on, Ford paid less attention to business and more attention to a hobby in which his new wealth allowed him to indulge. Ford had begun collecting historical memorabilia. He scoured junkyards across the United States, finding thousands of interesting artifacts.

His interest in business did not vanish completely, though. Over the course of the decade, he involved himself in everything from aviation to rubber plantations. Although most of his business ventures during this time did not prove profitable, Ford approached each one with the same savvy know-how that had brought him so much earlier success.

INVESTMENT IN ENERGY

In control of a vast empire, Ford investigated other areas of industry. He bought

coal fields and timber lands. The coal he mined and shipped to heat the furnaces of the Rouge plant. The timber he harvested for use in Model T frames.

Next, he got involved with electricity. He built a small power plant to generate electricity for his home at Fair Lane, and by 1921 he was sure that the use of electricity could be expanded into new and profitable industrial uses. So, when he heard about Muscle Shoals, a government water-power plant for sale in the Tennessee River Valley, he went to take a look at it.

Ford saw right away that the plant and dam the government had built across the Tennessee River could be renovated to prove profitable. The electricity the dam produced could be sold to industry, and water from the lake behind the dam could be sold as irrigation water for farms.

Thus, Ford proposed to pay the government $5 million, plus the cost of restoring the existing dam. He knew the project had already cost $85 million of taxpayer money, but he said that a quick sale of the property, even at a loss for the taxpayers, would pay for itself. The plant development would be good for the U.S. economy and a boon for agriculture in the states of Alabama and Tennessee.

The Wilson Dam on the Tennessee River, the site of Muscle Shoals.

"HENRY FOR PRESIDENT"

Ford's bid to purchase the plant interested a number of influential congressmen, who agreed that the project might benefit the area. But in 1922, politics called again, so, Ford put the Muscle Shoals project on hold and ran for president.

Ford's bid for office began when he was encouraged by the fund-raising efforts of a local "Henry for President" club, which had been formed in Dearborn in the spring of 1922. The club's members sold cardboard hats that read "We Want Henry," and used the money to start a letter-writing campaign on his behalf.

The hopes of people who wanted Ford to be president had some foundation. As a car manufacturer, Ford had nationwide name recognition, and, especially among industrial workers and farmers, he had a broad base of potential supporters. Biographer Booten Herndon writes, "He was the man who stood on the side of the worker. . . . Millions of Ford car owners transferred to him the kind of . . . affection they felt for the Model T. . . . Model T was the little man's car. First and last, Ford was the little man's man."[66]

THE NONEXISTENT FORD CAMPAIGN

Ford did not actually campaign for the presidential nomination, however. He told reporters that he regarded the Ford-for-president movement as "a joke only."[67] Nevertheless, by the spring of 1923 there were more than a thousand "Henry for President" clubs, and a number of journalists were taking the campaign seriously.

Some publications, including the *Wall Street Journal* and the *New York Times*, reported Ford's candidacy but did not offer an opinion on his qualifications. Two newspapers, the *Nation* and the *New Republic*, however, were clearly against his candidacy. A *New Republic* editorial, for example, evaluated Ford's understanding of money as "incomplete."[68] And Oswald Garrison Willard, a thirty-year veteran political analyst for the *Nation*, considered Ford's personality and character the greatest deterrent to his suitability for the presidency. "In no case," wrote Willard, "is there evidence that Mr. Ford ever has moments of contrition and repentance. He . . . apparently feels that he can do no wrong. . . . It is my deliberate belief that during [my years as a political writer] no candidate has been suggested [who is] so absolutely unfit for the White House as Henry Ford."[69]

Ford, for his part, contented himself with the publicity afforded him by the *Dearborn Independent*. He used its pages to propose an informal political platform and its columns to give his solutions for what he saw as the country's current economic problems—in particular, the lack of sufficient electrical energy, insufficient paper money, and reliance on the gold standard. He also quietly eliminated the anti-Semitic

A POEM FOR FORD THE PRESIDENTIAL CANDIDATE

During 1922, when Henry Ford was running for president of the United States, Witter Bynner wrote this campaign poem as an example of the appeal Ford had as a hardworking man. At the same time, Bynner wondered if Ford the rich industrialist had lost touch with the drudgery of his workers. The poem is quoted in David E. Nye's biography Henry Ford: "Ignorant Idealist."

"I met you for a moment, during the war,
A little gray man with an honest eye,
And on the tip of your nose—there at the very tip,
I see it still—was a bruise, a scab, a token.
You spoke of it yourself. 'It came,' you said,
'From studying a tractor wheel too close.'
Would you knock your nose again, as President?
Or would you enter through the eye of a needle,
Pulling the country after you like a thread,
Into a heaven made of smoke and brick,
With sweat for crowns and dinner pails for wings,
And living wages from the God of things?"

articles from the *Dearborn Independent*, publicizing, instead, the new worker-friendly five-day week at the Ford Motor Company.

A little less than a year before election day, however, Ford withdrew from the campaign. He gave no motive for his decision. His interest in Muscle Shoals also waned. After he dropped out of the campaign, the U.S. House of Representatives consented to Ford's offer of $5 million for Muscle Shoals, but the Senate failed to approve the measure. In October 1924, Ford withdrew his bid. In the end, Ford was relieved not to be involved in a government transaction or a campaign for public office. He told one interviewer, "We are not in politics and we are in business."[70]

A QUESTIONABLE RELATIONSHIP

While Ford was running for president, rumors began that he had become involved with his longtime secretary, Evangeline Coté, even though Coté married a man named Ray Dahlinger in 1917. Soon after Evangeline's son John Dahlinger was born on April 9, 1923, rumors questioned the child's parentage. People wondered if Ford, and not Ray Dahlinger, might be John's father.

Ford did nothing to thwart the rumors; in fact, his behavior encouraged them. He gave the Dahlingers the Ford family crib. The boy was christened in Henry Ford's own christening gown. And as John Dahlinger grew older, he began to call Henry Ford "Dad."

AN ORDINARY WIFE

In an interview with Henry Ford's wife, Clara, reporter Elizabeth Breuer was impressed by the woman's unpretentious appearance. This description of Mrs. Ford appears in Breuer's article "Henry Ford and the Believer," published in the Ladies Home Journal *in September 1923.*

"Riches had come to Mrs. Ford—riches beyond the imaginings of most . . . yet here sat a little, alert woman, past middle age, looking much younger than her years, and wearing what your mother is probably wearing at this moment—a little dark blue crêpe de chine [sheer silk] dress; you could buy its like in almost any department store, and for a modest sum; black silk stockings of rather heavy weave, and no finer than those you wear to work; conservatively cut black oxfords. An eyeglass hung on a piece of black ribbon; just think, not even on a chain of gold or platinum or diamonds, which she could certainly have had for the mere writing of a check; and on her well-formed wrist another piece of black grosgrain [closely woven] ribbon, binding a simple little watch.

I don't remember the color of Mrs. Ford's eyes. But they are dark and alert, wide open, with a lilt of brightness in them. They are appraising eyes, too, yet sweet eyes, and steady and clear. . . . [Her hair] is still dark brown, simply parted and combed back [from] Mrs. Ford's rounded face."

Henry Ford and his family attend a 1934 Detroit Tigers baseball game. From left to right: Edsel, Henry, grandchildren William and Josephine, and Eleanor Ford.

In the years to come, Evangeline remained one of the most visible people in Ford's life. She was put in charge of cataloging and organizing his rapidly growing collection of historical paraphernalia. Ford made public appearances with her, such as at baseball games. And he had their picture taken with Will Rogers and a number of other celebrities. "It was as if," says Lacey, "Henry regarded himself as being blessed by some special dispensation that rendered him immune to the ordinary rules of public conduct."[71]

FORD'S GRANDCHILDREN

Henry Ford also had four grandchildren, the third born within weeks of John Dahlinger. From the time the grandchildren were little, Edsel and wife Eleanor's children (Henry Ford II, born in 1917; Bensen Ford, born in 1919; Josephine Clay Ford, born in 1923; and William Clay Ford, born in 1925) spent a great deal of time at Fair Lane.

The grandchildren's love of Fair Lane reflected Ford's devotion to them and their interests. According to Henry Ford II's biographer Walter Hayes,

Henry Ford had given the boys their own half-acre farm on his property, where they raised their own crops, using equipment specially built to their own scale and size. . . . Henry Ford also built an enchanting Christmas cottage and filled it with toys every December. The boys were encouraged to use the entire estate as a sort of frontier post, camping out in barns and sleeping in haylofts. They . . . had rabbits and geese and chickens, and, in a small stable,

four Shetland ponies on which they rode. . . . The indoor swimming pool, the powerhouse, the bowling alley— there were no places considered out of bounds.[72]

Not surprisingly, Ford and the children's father shared their love of the children. Biographer Herndon describes one incident that shows this. "A designer who had an appointment with Edsel at the engineering laboratory was kept waiting for several hours. Finally Edsel and his father came in, their arms around each other's shoulders, talking earnestly. Edsel apologized to his visitor and

HENRY FORD IN THE KITCHEN

Henry Ford approved of appliances that made homemakers' work easier, but he felt that progress in food preparation had a long way to go toward helping women with limited time, skills, and education. He outlines his dream of cheap, ready-to-eat meals in My Philosophy of Industry.

"There is some machinery to use in the kitchen to-day. We have the vacuum cleaner, the various electric appliances, the electric washing machine, the electric ice boxes; but most of it is still too expensive. We must find some way to reduce the cost and some way to lighten the other labors of women. Many [meal preparation] processes have already been taken out of the home. Few housewives bake their own bread. You can buy better bread from the bakery now than many of the young women are able to make. . . .

Furthermore, the time will come when each member of the family can be given more individual attention; that is, each one can have the food that he likes and that is best suited for his growth. It may sound like an astounding proposition to advance, but we shall soon find a way to do much of the cooking outside and deliver it in a hot and appetizing condition at meal-time at no greater cost than that at which it is now being prepared in the workman's home."

Scores of Model Ts await shipment outside the Highland Park factory. Despite his father's belief to the contrary, Edsel Ford thought the Model T was outdated.

took him back to a small shop to show why he had forgotten the appointment. Father and son had been building a baby carriage for Edsel's daughter Josephine."[73]

THE PROBLEM OF THE MODEL T

In fact, Henry and Edsel Ford spent a great deal of time together. When separated, even briefly, they wrote letters and postcards and sent telegrams to each other. According to Lacey, "Scarcely a day went past that they did not spend several hours in each others' company, talking and working together on some project or other. When it was not possible for them to meet, they would talk on the telephone. A direct private line connected the study of Henry Ford at Fair Lane with that of Edsel on the other side of Detroit, and most evenings the line was busy."[74]

But the communications between Ford and his son were superficial. "In all these let-

ters and messages," Lacey writes, "so full of words and details, there is a lack of feeling. No serious issues are ever addressed. The children are well, the sun is shining, the car broke down, and the picnic was fun. . . . But if you did not know the identities of these two correspondents, [you would] never guess that there were many substantial business and personal issues on which they profoundly disagreed."[75]

One disagreement was about the Model T. Edsel had become increasingly aware that car buyers were interested in classy cars with more speed. Furthermore, he wanted to introduce hydraulic brakes instead of the mechanical brakes the Model T featured. With these things in mind, Edsel began suggesting that the Model T was outdated.

Edsel was right. The Model T was losing ground each month against its competitors. Yet Henry Ford could not bring himself to admit this. Thus, the Model T caused a deep rift between father and son. Ford employee

Charles Sorensen writes, "It was the Model T that drove a wedge between father and son, and . . . Edsel's desire for a change was one of the reasons Ford resisted its discontinuance."[76]

The disagreement lasted for nearly a decade and it had disastrous results. Ford belittled and bullied his son and eventually forced Edsel's friend Ernest Kanzler to resign. The stress also played a role in Edsel's developing stomach ulcers.

THE SAPIRO SUIT

In 1924, during the very early stages of Edsel's campaign to move beyond the Model T, Ford also revisited his anti-Semitic views. In a new round of articles, Ford accused the Jews of plotting to seize control of U.S. agriculture and of cheating American farmers.

These anti-Semitic views were once again printed where they were easiest to place, in the *Dearborn Independent*. This time, however, Ford and editor William J. Cameron sharpened the attack to point to one Jewish man in particular: lawyer Aaron Sapiro, a former rabbi who had been working to form groups of Midwest farms into cooperatives, a business enterprise that allows farmers to deal with customers directly rather than through a third party. Sapiro believed that farmers should control their own prices, rather than be controlled by the market. Ford considered the Midwest farmers' allegiance to the cooperatives to be the cause of their not supporting his presidential bid, and he blamed Sapiro for this. There was no evidence to prove Ford's claim, however, so Sapiro sued Henry Ford for $1 million, charging him with defamation of character.

The trial took some time to come to court. Ford was ordered to appear on April 1, 1927. He did not make it to court, however, because he was injured in a car accident the evening before his scheduled appearance. Ultimately, the Sapiro case was settled privately out of court. Ford retracted all attacks on Sapiro and apologized for everything he had said against the Jews in general. He also closed down the *Dearborn Independent* permanently.

The reasons for Ford's decision to settle the case are unclear, but some people believe it was the result of dishonest behavior on the part of Ford and his attorneys. Case records show that Ford's lawyers could have been accused of jury tampering, and newspaper reports said that Ford staged his car crash to get out of appearing in court. Thus, some biographers contend that Ford was insincere in his apology to Sapiro. Lacey writes,

> The sheer intellectual unworthiness of blaming the world's problems on a nonexistent clique of conspirators determined the dishonest and unworthy way that it all ended: the staged car crash, the jury tampering, and the apology that was not an apology at all, since Henry Ford clung to his prejudice privately and not always so privately for the rest of his life.[77]

INNOVATIONS IN AVIATION

While Henry Ford dealt with the Sapiro suit, Edsel Ford became interested in building airplanes. Edsel wanted to redesign the wooden airplanes of the time and make them of metal. He foresaw the development of commercial uses for airplanes and the establishment of regular national and international airmail routes. With these ideas in mind, Edsel authorized the planning of an aviation field.

In 1924 the Ford Motor Company moved forward with this project, taking a giant step in the direction of modern air freight and air travel. Edsel established a state-of-the-art runway three hundred feet wide and thirty-seven hundred feet long. Hangars and shops were built to house and maintain aircraft. Then the company issued an open invitation to private and military planes to use the field. According to Nevins and Hill, the runway "was one of the finest in the world."[78]

Henry Ford supported his son's idea, and to demonstrate the feasibility of commercial air flights, Ford started a flying service between Detroit and Chicago. These flights proved the reliability and speed of the planes the Ford Motor Company was developing and showed that Ford was a leader in the aviation industry.

Henry Ford receives the Grand Cross of the German Eagle from German diplomats in 1938. Despite the closure of the Dearborn Independent *in 1927, Ford clung to his anti-Semitic views throughout his life.*

THE FUTURE OF AVIATION

For a few years in the 1920s, the Ford Motor Company invested in the new airplane industry. Biographer Garet Garrett, a friend of Ford's, recorded Ford's vision of aviation's future in The Wild Wheel.

"[Ford asked] if I had any reservations about the future of flying, I acknowledged a few.

'You shouldn't,' he said. 'You shouldn't. And do you know why you shouldn't?'

'Why?' I asked.

'Because so many young people are putting thought material into it. When you see that you may be sure that something big is coming out of it. . . .'

I said: 'On the ground, before there were any automobiles, you saw streets full of them. Now what do you see in the sky?'

Speaking slowly, . . . he said: 'Many planes. Many, many planes.'"

In 1927, Ford started two airmail routes, one between Detroit and Chicago and one between Detroit and Cleveland. Flying quickly became popular throughout the United States and, in 1927, airplanes put in more than 260,000 air miles. By 1928, Ford had thirty-six tri-motor planes under construction. The following year, Ford sold eighty-six planes, which were highly improved in structural design and had the ability to fly up to 164 miles per hour.

Despite its promise, however, Ford's aviation business was not profitable. More than any other segment of the Ford business, the aviation department lost money. Then when the Great Depression began in 1929, plunging the United States into economic chaos, airplane sales dropped off almost completely. As a result, the aviation operation was dropped in 1932, with a total operating and construction deficit of more than $16 million.

RUBBER EMPIRE IN BRAZIL

Another area Ford got involved with during the time was rubber production in Brazil. At the time, the Far Eastern country of Malaysia had a monopoly on rubber. This made it possible for rubber producers there to raise their prices, which would make latex, a type of rubber used to make automobile tires, very expensive. Convinced that his company would be unable to pay for enough Far Eastern rubber to make its tires, Ford looked for another place to grow his own rubber. He settled on Brazil, a South American country whose rubber industry had been crippled by the Malaysian monopoly.

In 1927 the government of Brazil sold Ford 300,000 acres on the Tapajos River (in northern Brazil) for the project. Two years later, fourteen hundred acres of that land had been cleared for the planting of rubber seedlings. In addition, a small city, called Fordlandia, was built to house the people who would work the rubber plantation. It included rainproof worker homes, sanitation facilities, and schools.

But Fordlandia and the rubber plantation ultimately failed. There were two primary reasons for this. First, Ford did not choose a suitable site for the plantation, and many trees died because of disease. Second, Ford refused to hire Brazilian managers who understood the people. The managers Ford did hire antagonized the Brazilian workers by insisting they live in company housing. University professor Carl D. LaRue writes, "[The workers] didn't like those galvanized iron bake ovens [with] . . . showers. [They] normally had a palm-thatched shack and they could swim in the river. They didn't need the showers and they didn't like those hot, little houses."[79]

However in two ways, Fordlandia was successful. During its short existence, the plantation produced enough rubber to offset the anticipated rubber shortage. It also succeeded as a research project. Rubber plantation owners discovered that Brazilian rubber trees had a relatively short maturing period of fourteen years, in comparison with the twenty-two years required in Malaysia.

THE 15-MILLIONTH MODEL T

As the 1920s came to a close, Ford realized that he had to discontinue the Model T; sales were down and Ford was losing money. Despite his previous conviction that he could manufacture the same car year after year, on November 25, 1927, the

Workers tap rubber trees at the Fordlandia rubber plantation in northern Brazil.

THE COST OF RETOOLING

In Today and Tomorrow, *Henry Ford gives a brief account of what it meant financially to retool his factory in order to switch from making the Model T to making the Model A.*

"We set a date [May 26, 1927] to begin changing over [from Model T to Model A production]. The planning department had to calculate on just the amount of material which would keep production going at full speed until that date and then permit production to stop without having any material [left] over. It had to make the same calculations for our thirty-two associated plants and for the forty-two branches.

In the meantime, hundreds of drawings had to be made by the engineers for the building of the new dies [cutting and shaping devices] and tools. We arranged to make this change without a wholesale shut down. We 'staggered' the process, changing one department at a time, so that by the time the last change was made production had caught up to the last department involved.

All of this sounds simple enough, but here is what it meant to make only eighty-one [of the six thousand] changes. We had to design 4,759 punch and dies and 4,243 jigs and fixtures. We had to build 5,622 punch and dies and 6,990 jigs and fixtures. The labor cost of this amounted to $5,682,387, while the material ran to $1,395,596. Installing new enamel ovens at thirteen branches cost $371,000, and changing the equipment in twenty-nine branches cost $145,650. That is to say, these [eighty-one] changes cost us upward of eight million dollars, not estimating time lost from production."

Ford Motor Company announced that the Model T plant would be reorganized to accommodate the manufacture of a new motor car. That car, a new Model A, was already in the planning stage.

The following day, November 26, 1927, the 15-millionth Model T came off the assembly line and had its picture taken. Biographer Charles Merz describes the moment:

No brass bands played the national anthem, no symphonies were composed, and no press association bulletins rushed the news across the country.

For Model T was an antique now. The times had passed it by, and this was Götterdämmerung [the last hurrah] for the high-hearted little box of tin that had held its own on the open road since the dawn of an age of motors.[80]

It was time for Henry Ford and the Ford Motor Company to move on to something else.

Chapter

7 How It All Became History

In Ford's later years, he rested considerably on his former success but continued to have a say in his company's business ventures. With the demise of the Model T, he turned his attention to bigger and better cars.

Even as they worked together to build these new cars, Ford and his son, Edsel, never really got along. In fact, instead of working through problems with Edsel, Ford often relied more on his employees—in particular, a man named Harry Bennett—for advice and support. Until almost the very end, Ford remained certain that his control of the company was the only way to keep it moving ahead.

THE NEW MODEL A AND THE V-8

The retooling of the Model T factory took several months. When it did reopen and produce the new Model A, Ford was not satisfied. As popular as the Model A was, it did not sell enough cars to pay for the factory's renovation.

In response, Ford applied his cure for sagging sales. He cut prices for the Model A and raised wages. At first, sales went up, but not enough. Next, he raised prices and laid off workers. Still the car did not make money.

Finally, Ford realized that a new criterion had entered people's decision to buy a car. Durability and reliability were not enough anymore. People wanted style. Thus, Ford suggested a more stylish and more powerful car to replace the Model A. Ultimately, he chose to develop a car with an eight-cylinder engine, an innovation that would

Henry Ford (left) and Edsel Ford. The father and son disagreed on how the Ford Motor Company should operate.

make the car faster and stronger than any he had built before.

The first public showing of the eight-cylinder car, the Ford V-8, on March 28, 1932, brought many new buyers to Ford. Its powerful motor and sporty look were popular, and sales increased. But even the V-8 did not restore the company to first place in auto sales.

REDISTRIBUTING WEALTH

While Ford continued trying to sell more cars, most Americans found themselves unable to make a living. The Great Depression had already lasted three years, and very few people had jobs.

After Franklin D. Roosevelt was elected president in 1932, he introduced the New

Despite offering more power than earlier engines, the Ford V-8 (pictured, foreground) failed to advance the company to first place in auto sales.

HUNTING UP THE OLD STUFF

When Ford was building his "living history" museum, Greenfield Village, he wanted to find things that he himself had used when he lived on his family's farm. This account of one of his finds appears in Robert Lacey's biography Ford: The Men and the Machine.

"Henry Ford started a search for the little steam engine he had steered around the Michigan countryside in the summer of '82 [1882]. He could remember its serial number, 345, and with the help of the Westinghouse Company, he eventually tracked it down to a farm in Pennsylvania, where it was languishing, decrepit and rusting. Henry had the machine repaired, oiled, and polished, brought it back to Dearborn, put water in the boiler, stoked up the fire—and threshed with it again on his sixtieth birthday. . . .

This was the happiest period of Henry Ford's life, and he would hark back to those years increasingly as he got older. His search for old 345, sending out his agents to scour the countryside regardless of expense, was, in some ways, a search for his own youth, a quest for the fresh and innocent Henry Ford that the successful, hard-nosed industrialist had lost sight of."

Deal, a strategy to redistribute national wealth and improve the lives of Americans hit hard by the depression. The New Deal would accomplish this by introducing progressively higher income tax brackets for the wealthy. The tax money collected would then be used to house, feed, clothe, and put to work America's poor people. Henry Ford's new bracket would call for him to pay up to a third or more of his profits in taxes.

Ford, however, did not want to pay the extra taxes. Thus, following the passage of Roosevelt's income tax laws, Ford looked for a way to get out of paying taxes on his family's income. His solution was forming a charitable organization (charities are tax exempt) and then donating 95 percent of his assets to it. The organization was called

the Ford Foundation. Its purpose was to advance the causes of many nonprofit and educational institutions. By setting up this foundation, Ford diverted $321 million in taxes from Roosevelt's redistribution plan into his own project.

GREENFIELD VILLAGE AND THE HENRY FORD MUSEUM

Two other projects Ford worked on during this time were connected to his interest in historical paraphernalia. By 1933, in his seventieth year, Ford had spent a decade collecting memorabilia. That year, he completed construction of and dedicated an eight-acre museum in Dearborn, called the

Henry Ford Museum, to house the memorabilia. His friend, inventor Thomas Edison, presided at the opening ceremonies.

On an adjoining ten acres, Ford also dedicated Greenfield Village, a living history exhibit. Greenfield Village eventually included more than one hundred restored buildings, such as Thomas Edison's Menlo Park, New Jersey, workshop and the little white farmhouse where Ford was born. Removed from their original sites and rebuilt near Fair Lane, the buildings became a popular tourist attraction.

UNIONS GAIN POWER

While Ford had been traveling around to antique shops finding items to add to his historical collections, the United States had seen a new entity enter the industrial scene. Labor unions, seeking to give workers higher wages and better benefits, were gaining power. In 1935, Congress passed the National Labor Relations Act. This law cleared the way for labor unions to solicit membership among factory workers by distributing leaflets and holding organizational meetings inside plants like Ford's.

Ford, however, was not a union supporter. Whenever the issue of labor unions came up, Ford pointed out that his workers had better treatment than the workers in any unionized plant. Ford was convinced that he knew what was best for his employees. According to former employee Lee Iacocca, "Ford considered unions entirely unnecessary—who, after all, knew more about taking care of his people than he?"[81]

WHAT THE UNIONS WANTED

Initially, the unions were unsuccessful at Ford. Although union organizers had an ally in Edsel, who believed in giving his workers a voice, Ford's new personnel director, Harry Herbert Bennett, had no such leanings. Bennett had the personality of a tough policeman, and he took a hard-line stance against the union. This supported Ford's views and made Bennett the person from whom Ford sought advice.

In 1937, two years after the passage of the National Labor Relations Act, a labor union called the United Auto Workers (UAW) signed contracts with two of the biggest automobile manufacturers, General Motors and Chrysler, allowing workers at those plants to unionize. Next, the UAW hoped to organize the workers in the Ford plant.

On May 26, 1937, union organizers began their campaign. Confident, they marched toward the Ford factory, where they planned to hand out pamphlets. Before they arrived, though, the men were attacked and beaten by thugs hired by Harry Bennett. This type of violence continued during the summer of 1937, and Ford battled union organizers for the next four years.

THE UNION PROVES ITS POWER

Things finally changed on April 1, 1941. That day, fifteen hundred of Ford's Rouge plant workers staged a strike that turned violent. Strikers tried to keep other workers from entering the plant, and a riot started.

This time, Edsel prevailed, although not by his own efforts. His mother, Clara Ford, used her influence with Henry Ford to turn the tide in favor of the union. Says Brough,

> Clara had come around to sharing her son's point of view. . . . The seventy-four year old woman [said that] unless [Henry Ford] made peace with the union, men would die. . . . She refused to see that happen. If the [union] contract was not signed, she would run away, abandon [Henry], and their marriage would be ended.[82]

In June 1941, Henry Ford gave in to his wife's demand. He signed the settlement with the United Auto Workers, allowing his workers to unionize. However, as Lacey writes, this was a disappointment for Ford: "[Ford] appears seriously to have cherished the expectation, in the spring of 1941, that his men would, in a gesture of confidence and gratitude for his lifetime of laboring on their behalf, reject [the union] . . . and vote instead to make Ford a non-union shop."[83]

THE CAUSE OF DEFENSE

World events soon turned Ford's attention away from union activity at the Ford plant. Since 1939, Germany's Adolf Hitler had been waging a fierce war with most of Europe. This fact motivated some of Ford's European plants to convert to war production, and the Ford plant in Windsor, Canada, began making small tanks for Great Britain.

Initially maintaining the stance he had pursued before World War I, Ford opposed entering the war in Europe. However, as the

The 1941 Rogue River strike (above) turned violent (left) when nonstriking auto workers tried to enter the plant.

hostilities escalated, he authorized a new $65 million airplane plant to be built near the Rouge. The plant, called Willow Run after a stream that meandered through the area, manufactured steel castings for airplanes and tanks at the rate of three hundred per day. Soon after, Ford contracted to make 4,236 airplane engines. This order, says biographer William Adams Simonds, was "the largest single airplane-engine contract let [assigned] under the [defense] program up to that time."[84]

Ford then participated in two other defense efforts. First, he reopened the Highland Park plant to make tanks called M-4s. Second, he founded military training schools for the navy, air force, and army.

Public support for the defense effort was strong, and Ford's part in military preparedness was much publicized and approved. Opinion polls showed that, even though General Motors and Chrysler were also contributing, to most people Ford represented the primary domestic defense effort.

A Practical Problem Solver

In Henry Ford: "Ignorant Idealist" *biographer David E. Nye discusses Ford's practical problem-solving skills.*

"The hallmark of [Ford's] imagination was this ability to get at the root of a problem while maintaining at the same time a larger view of its relations to other problems. Thus, if farmers would not sell their crops, industry must find uses for them, or both would fail. If men were unhealthy, then they must find new foods and adopt more abstemious diets. If the economy faltered or workers went on strike, then parasites, bankers, or a conspiracy must be the cause, and a new basis for monetary value was the solution. . . .

A man of unusual self-assurance, he relied upon his intuitions, as his mind jumped from one subject to another very strikingly. Never at a loss for words, he spoke in a fluent and simple vocabulary, typically in very short, telegraphic type sentences. His mind was quick, and he seldom needed to be taught, or told, a thing twice. He exerted a kind of magnetism, which may be partially explained by his assurance, simplicity, and intelligence, but which resists complete explanation. . . .

And yet, . . . his was a mind admirably suited to solving the technical problems encountered in building an automobile. Like [the inventor Thomas Alva] Edison, Ford was tireless, made no *a priori* [unanalyzed] assumptions about what might work, and would try every conceivable possibility."

Former German leader Adolph Hitler reads a newspaper. Henry Ford suffered a second stroke after learning that articles from the Dearborn Independent *had been widely distributed throughout Hitler's Germany.*

A DOWNTURN IN HEALTH

Ford's business success during this time was accompanied by a decline in his general health. This decline stretched back several years. In 1932, he recovered from surgery for a hernia. Six years later, in 1938, he suffered a stroke, which caused him some loss of memory and mobility, but again he recovered well.

In 1941, however, nearing eighty years of age, Ford had a second stroke, from which he recovered more slowly. This one seemed to be brought on by a revelation that there had been wide distribution in Hitler's Ger-

many of anti-Semitic articles from the *Dearborn Independent*. Hitler was violently anti-Semitic, and much of his governmental policy centered around ridding the world of Jews. Biographer Robert Lacey contends that Ford's having to face the fact that his newspaper activity had contributed to Hitler's violence was overwhelming: "Newsreel film showing the opening of the [German] concentration camps was brought to the factory . . . and when Henry Ford . . . was confronted with the atrocities which finally and unanswerably laid bare the bestiality of the prejudice to which he had contributed, he collapsed with [his second] stroke."[85]

EDSEL'S HEALTH DECLINES

Edsel Ford also experienced a downturn in health during this period. Edsel worked hard during this time and rested very little. This stress, combined with his father's belittling disapproval, served to weaken Edsel's health.

Henry Ford was unable to see that Edsel's health problems were serious, however. Perhaps his own hardiness blinded him. He had exercised vigorously all his life, eaten healthy foods, refused to drink or smoke, and at seventy-nine was recovering from his second stroke.

During 1942, Ford took his disapproval of Edsel one step further. He began to speak of turning the company over to a new president, one who was more to his liking, Harry Bennett. This caused his son even more tension.

In January 1942, Edsel had a second surgery for stomach ulcers. But the problem was more serious than ulcers. According to Herndon, "Ulcers were gnawing at his belly. . . . And cancer was developing in his bowels. He was a very sick man. . . . His frequent hospitalization, his very appearance as he gauntly tried to carry on, increased the old man's hostility."[86]

EDSEL DIES

On May 26, 1943, Edsel died. Henry Ford was grief-stricken, but he could not acknowledge his part in Edsel's death.

The death of Edsel at forty-nine "sent a wave of sorrow through Detroit and Dearborn," say Nevins and Hill, "for all who knew Edsel loved him."[87] Ford employees grieved openly. Biographer Simonds reports that "on the afternoon of the funeral as the services began . . . workers laid down their tools in Ford factories from England to Australia. At the bomber plant [Willow Run], the chatter of rivet guns was silenced."[88]

COMPANY PRESIDENT AGAIN

Following Edsel's death, the Ford Motor Company was left without a president. Ford however, was determined to return, and he proved successful. On June 1, 1943, at a meeting of the board of directors, Henry Ford was reelected president. Simonds writes, "Once more [Ford] picked up the reins he had handed over to his son twenty-five years earlier."[89]

Ford was nearly eighty, though, and his mind was not what it once was. Furthermore, Ford turned more often to Harry Bennett during this time, a decision that did not prove beneficial to the company. According to biographer Herndon,

> In the midst of a war, with huge military orders to fill, Henry Ford himself assumed the presidency of the company. He was not fit for the task. In effect he had no lieutenants, for the only man on whom he chose to lean was Bennett, [a man] more interested in personal power than in production.[90]

Despite this, the Ford Motor Company survived Ford's second presidency because of war production. Says Iacocca, "If World War II hadn't turned the company's manufacturing prowess to the business of making B-24 bombers and jeeps, it is entirely possible that the . . . V-8 engine might have been Ford's last innovation."[91]

FORD GIVES UP CONTROL

Ford maintained his position for a little over two years. During that time, his health deteriorated and his physician declared that he was too frail to come to the plant. As a result, Ford increasingly gave Bennett blanket responsibilities.

As Bennett became more powerful, rumors of his possible presidency circulated. When they reached Eleanor Ford, Edsel's widow, she reacted strongly. Both Eleanor and Clara Ford were determined to see one of Edsel's sons, not Harry Bennett, succeed

---

FORD'S SUBSTITUTE SON

In Ford: Decline and Rebirth, 1933–1962, *authors Allan Nevins and Frank Ernest Hill discuss the affinity between Henry Ford and Harry Herbert Bennett.*

"In many respects, as the years passed, [Harry] Bennett became something near a substitute son to Henry Ford, and a spoiled son at that; for Henry's relations with Edsel did not improve. When Edsel's brother-in-law and co-planner Ernest Kanzler was abruptly ejected [fired], close observers had been startled by the sudden glimpse of a deep gulf opening between father and son. That gulf remained. Despite all Edsel's forbearing loyalty, relations between them could never again be quite the same. Edsel's wife remonstrated with the old man, Clara was deeply troubled, and Edsel's own grief was often clear. Far from seeing that the son's superb tolerance, combined with his determination to continue struggling for a more progressive administration, really proved his strength, the father in a growing conviction of Edsel's weakness turned to Bennett as the tough, realistic, hard-hitting type he had wished Edsel to be. And as Bennett became a daily companion, earning Henry's approval at every turn, he achieved the status of lieutenant, son, and crony combined. Henry telephoned him early every morning, often carried [drove] him to work, and telephoned him again nearly every evening at nine-thirty. He took any criticism of Bennett's policies, alleged dishonesty, and violent acts, as criticism of his own management; and as it was hard to tell where one authority ended and the other began, he was at least partly right."

Henry Ford as president of the company. Nevins and Hill write,

> Edsel's wife had not watched her husband's years of suffering, and heard his anguished denunciations of Bennett, without resolving that her son's rights should be respected. . . . [Likewise,] Clara, as close observers noted, had been expostulating [reasoning] with Henry, denouncing Bennett as persecutor of her son and evil genius of the plant, and taking Mrs. Edsel Ford's side in insisting that the grandsons be trained for control. Both were women of character whose self-assertion now counted. [92]

Henry Ford paid little attention to business after his retirement in 1945.

The women's voice prevailed. On August 10, 1943, Ford's grandson, Henry Ford II, came home from the navy. A year later, on August 10, 1944, he was named executive vice president. The next year, on September 21, 1945, Henry Ford submitted his resignation to the board of directors and twenty-eight-year-old Henry Ford II was elected president of Ford Motor Company.

One of the first things the new president did was fire Harry Bennett. Less than three months later, he hired a new administrative team of ten experts in cost analysis, price control, and management skills. According to Simonds, the young president was good for the company: "Assumption of command by Henry Ford II ushered in a new era, in which fresh vigor and youth brought sweeping changes." [93]

"A Tired Old Man"

After September 21, 1945, Ford paid little attention to the business. He was, says Harry Bennett, "just a tired old man who wanted to live in peace." [94] Relieved, finally, of any sense of responsibility for the company, Ford and his wife settled into retirement.

On April 6, 1947, after a vacation in Virginia, the Fords returned home to Dearborn. They could not have arrived on a worse day, for a rainstorm had flooded the Fair Lane generators and cut off their electricity, leaving the house chilled except in front of the fireplaces. Tired and without time to adjust to the damp chill of Michigan, they slept in the unheated house. The next morning, April 7, 1947, Ford ate a breakfast cooked over the fireplace and

Mourners view the body of Henry Ford in April 1947.

then insisted on being taken for a ride to visit his parents' graves. He returned in good spirits, but did not feel well.

That night, Clara and Fair Lane's maid, Rosa Buhler, sat with Ford as he tried to sleep. The chauffeur left the house in search of a working telephone and called the doctor. But Ford could not breathe. He died of a massive stroke before midnight before the doctor arrived.

MOURNED BY MULTITUDES

The public's response to Ford's death showed how much positive feedback a powerful industrialist can command. On April 9, 1947, a hundred thousand people passed before his open coffin to pay their respects. Obituaries appeared in major newspapers throughout the country. The writers were mostly kind to him, without totally overlooking his prejudices. As Lacey wrote, "If you were not Jewish, had not been beaten up by an [anti-union] squad, and were not a friend or relative of Edsel Ford, you felt that your own life had been touched directly by Henry Ford and had been touched for the better, on the whole." [95]

St. Paul's Cathedral in Detroit held the funeral services on April 10. Twenty thousand

Pallbearers lift Henry Ford's casket into a Packard hearse outside Detroit's St. Paul's Cathedral.

people gathered at the church to pay tribute to the man who brought the car to the ordinary person. In Detroit, all city offices closed at noon, City Hall was draped in black, and city buses stopped for a moment of silence. In Dearborn, businesses remained closed. And as Ford's body was carried to a cemetery near Fair Lane (in a Packard hearse because none of the Ford automobiles was big enough to carry a casket), the nurses at Ford Hospital lined up outside in their uniforms.

Nine years after Ford's death, the Ford Foundation offered its Ford Motor Company stock to the public; that is, ordinary people could buy stock in Henry Ford's family enterprise. The stocks sold well and earned the Ford Foundation $640 million. As Lacey writes, "The national stampede to buy into [Ford's] company was America's final, colossal tribute to the magic in his name—the sincerest tribute of all, since it was expressed in terms of dollars."[96]

Notes

Chapter 1: Farm Mechanic

1. George H. Holmes, *The Reminiscences of Mr. George H. Holmes*. Dearborn, MI: Ford Motor Company Archives Oral History Section, 1954, p. 12.
2. James Brough, *The Ford Dynasty: An American Story*. New York: Doubleday, 1977, p. 31.
3. Brough, *The Ford Dynasty*, p. 31.
4. Margaret Ford Ruddiman, "Memories of My Brother Henry Ford," *Michigan History*, September 1953, p. 241.
5. Robert Lacey, *Ford: The Men and the Machine*. Boston: Little, Brown, 1986, p. 9.
6. Rose Wilder Lane, *Henry Ford's Own Story*. New York: Ellis O. Jones, 1917, pp. 8–9.
7. Lacey, *Ford*, p. 25.
8. Charles Merz, *And Then Came Ford*. New York: Doubleday, Doran, 1929, p. 30.
9. Brough, *The Ford Dynasty*, p. 36.
10. Holmes, *The Reminiscences of Mr. George H. Holmes*, p. 6.
11. Roger Burlingame, *Henry Ford: A Great Life in Brief*. New York: Alfred A. Knopf, 1964, p. 19.
12. Quoted in Lacey, *Ford*, p. 23.
13. Peter Collier and David Horowitz, *The Fords: An American Epic*. New York: Summit Books, 1987, p. 25.
14. Quoted in Lacey, *Ford*, p. 26.
15. Lacey, *Ford*, p. 26.
16. Quoted in Elizabeth Breuer, "Henry Ford and the Believer," *Ladies Home Journal*, September 1923, p. 124.
17. Collier and Horowitz, *The Fords*, p. 27.
18. Henry Ford, in collaboration with Samuel Crowther, *My Life and Work*. New York: Garden City Publishing, 1922, p. 26.

Chapter 2: Better than Steam

19. Ford, *My Life and Work*, p. 28.
20. Ford, *My Life and Work*, p. 30.
21. Quoted in Brough, *The Ford Dynasty*, p. 41.
22. Lacey, *Ford*, p. 27.
23. Merz, *And Then Came Ford*, p. 51.
24. Ford, *My Life and Work*, p. 31.
25. Quoted in Lacey, *Ford*, p. 48.
26. Lacey, *Ford*, p. 50.
27. Burlingame, *Henry Ford*, p. 33.
28. Upton Sinclair, *The Flivver King*. Detroit, MI: United Automobile Workers of America, 1937, p. 11.
29. Burlingame, *Henry Ford*, p. 33.
30. Burlingame, *Henry Ford*, p. 34.
31. Allan Nevins, *Ford: The Times, the Man, the Company*. New York: Charles Scribner's Sons, 1954, pp. 242–43.
32. Nevins, *Ford*, p. 243.
33. Lacey, *Ford*, p. 74.

Chapter 3: Cars from A to T

34. Lacey, *Ford*, p. 77.
35. Brough, *The Ford Dynasty*, p. 64.
36. Anne Jardim, *The First Henry Ford: A Study in Personality and Business Leadership*. Cambridge, MA: MIT Press, 1970, p. 243.
37. Lacey, *Ford*, p. 78.
38. Lacey, *Ford*, p. 78.
39. Quoted in Lacey, *Ford*, p. 84.
40. Lacey, *Ford*, p. 82.
41. Brough, *The Ford Dynasty*, p. 67.
42. Quoted in Brough, *The Ford Dynasty*, p. 70.
43. Nevins, *Ford*, p. 390.
44. Nevins, *Ford*, p. 391.

Chapter 4: The Millionaire

45. Nevins, *Ford*, pp. 392–93.
46. Keith Sward, *The Legend of Henry Ford*. New York: Rinehart, 1948, p. 34.

47. Lacey, *Ford*, p. 110.

48. Sward, *The Legend of Henry Ford*, p. 36.

49. Brough, *The Ford Dynasty*, pp. 16–17.

50. Burlingame, *Henry Ford*, pp. 80–81.

51. *Literary Digest*, "The Rise of Henry Ford," February 24, 1917, p. 498.

52. Lacey, *Ford*, p. 185.

53. Quoted in Lacey, *Ford*, p. 225.

54. Burlingame, *Henry Ford*, p. 82.

55. Burlingame, *Henry Ford*, p. 83.

56. Sward, *The Legend of Henry Ford*, p. 40.

Chapter 5: Conflict and Control

57. Quoted in Judson F. Welliver, "Henry Ford, Dreamer and Worker," *American Review of Reviews*, November 1923, p. 481.

58. Welliver, "Henry Ford, Dreamer and Worker," p. 487.

59. Garet Garrett, *The Wild Wheel*. New York: Pantheon Books, 1952, p. 97.

60. Quoted in Welliver, "Henry Ford, Dreamer and Worker," p. 482.

61. Quoted in Welliver, "Henry Ford, Dreamer and Worker," p. 495.

62. Allan Nevins and Frank Ernest Hill, *Ford: Expansion and Challenge, 1915–1933*. New York: Charles Scribner's Sons, 1957, p. 113.

63. Nevins and Hill, *Ford: Expansion and Challenge*, p. 272.

64. Quoted in Nevins and Hill, *Ford: Expansion and Challenge*, p. 276.

65. Nevins and Hill, *Ford: Expansion and Challenge*, p. 276.

Chapter 6: New Directions

66. Booten Herndon, *Ford: An Unconventional Biography of the Men and Their Times*. New York: Weybright and Talley, 1969, pp. 163–64.

67. Quoted in *Literary Digest*, "The Latest Ford 'Joke,'" May 6, 1916, p. 1,267.

68. *New Republic*, "Ford and Ideas," October 21, 1923, p. 249.

69. Oswald Garrison Willard, "Why Henry Should Not Be President," *Nation*, May 30, 1923, p. 623.

70. Quoted in Nevins and Hill, *Ford: Expansion and Challenge*, p. 311.

71. Lacey, *Ford*, p. 227.

72. Walter Hayes, *Henry: A Life of Henry Ford II*. New York: Grove Weidenfeld, 1990, p. 8.

73. Herndon, *Ford*, pp. 144–45.

74. Lacey, *Ford*, p. 260.

75. Lacey, *Ford*, p. 261.

76. Quoted in Herndon, *Ford*, p. 141.

77. Lacey, *Ford*, pp. 217–18.

78. Nevins and Hill, *Ford: Expansion and Challenge*, p. 240.

79. Carl D. LaRue, *The Reminiscences of Mr. Carl D. LaRue*. Dearborn, MI: Ford Motor Company Archives Oral History Section, 1955, pp. 39–40.

80. Merz, *And Then Came Ford*, p. 292.

Chapter 7: How It All Became History

81. Lee Iacocca, "Driving Force: Henry Ford," *Time*, December 7, 1998, p. 79.

82. Brough, *The Ford Dynasty*, p. 215.

83. Lacey, *Ford*, p. 377.

84. William Adams Simonds, *Henry Ford: His Life, His Work, His Genius*. Los Angeles: Floyd Clymer, 1946, p. 298.

85. Lacey, *Ford*, pp. 218–19.

86. Herndon *Ford*, p. 175.

87. Allan Nevins and Frank Ernest Hill, *Ford: Decline and Rebirth, 1933–1962*. New York: Charles Schribner's Sons, 1962, p. 248.

88. Simonds, *Henry Ford*, p. 338.

89. Simonds, *Henry Ford*, p. 338.

90. Herndon, *Ford*, p. 176.

91. Iacocca, "Driving Force: Henry Ford," p. 79.

92. Nevins and Hill, *Ford: Decline and Rebirth*, p. 250.

93. Simonds, *Henry Ford*, p. 139.

94. Quoted in Lacey, *Ford*, p. 442.

95. Lacey, *Ford*, p. 448.

96. Lacey, *Ford*, p. 454.

For Further Reading

Books

Hazel B. Aird and Catherine Ruddiman, *Henry Ford: Young Man with Ideas*. New York: Macmillan, 1960. Henry Ford's niece uses the memories of Margaret Ford Ruddiman (Henry Ford's sister) to fashion these stories of the childhood and early achievements of the successful industrialist.

James P. Barry, *Henry Ford and Mass Production: An Inventor Builds a Car That Millions Can Afford*. New York: Franklin Watts, 1973. Focuses on the development of the Ford Motor Company and its effect on manufacturing practices.

Catherine Gourley, *Wheels of Time: A Biography of Henry Ford*. Brookfield, CT: Millbrook Press, 1997. This biographical essay explains Ford's impact on the concept of time in the twentieth century.

Jacqueline L. Harris, *Henry Ford*. New York: Franklin Watts, 1984. An overall picture of the man and his achievements.

Paul Joseph, *Inventors: Henry Ford*. Minneapolis, MN: ABDO & Daughters, 1997. Easy-to-read survey of Ford's life, with illustrations and a glossary.

Regina Zimmerman Kelly, *Henry Ford*. Chicago: Follett, 1970. Many personalizing details fill out this picture of Henry Ford and the impact of his work on U.S. culture.

Michael Pollard, *Henry Ford and Ford*. Watford, Hertfordshire, England: Exley Publications, 1995. Elegantly illustrated history of the development of Henry Ford's automobile plant and its impact on the twentieth century.

Website

Henry Ford Museum and Greenfield Village (www.hfmgv.org). This website provides much information about the indoor/outdoor museum, including online tours.

Works Consulted

Books

Norman Brauer, *There to Breathe the Beauty.* Dalto, PA: Norman Braver Publications, 1995. This book includes itineraries, pictures, and excerpts from journals detailing Henry Ford's camping trips between 1915 and 1924.

James Brough, *The Ford Dynasty: An American Story.* New York: Doubleday, 1977. Subtitled "The saga of the family that pioneered the automobile industry," this study emphasizes the relationships among members of the Ford family.

Roger Burlingame, *Henry Ford: A Great Life in Brief.* New York: Alfred A. Knopf, 1964. Considered one of the more balanced studies of Ford and his company.

Peter Collier and David Horowitz, *The Fords: An American Epic.* New York: Summit Books, 1987. Overall picture of the Ford Motor Company in the context of U.S. and world industry.

Ford Motor Company, *Ford at Fifty.* New York: Simon and Schuster, 1953. A company view of the Fords, with many great photos.

Henry Ford, *The International Jew.* London: G.F. Green, 1948. Private publication of edited and abridged copies of articles that appeared in Ford's newspaper, *The Dearborn Independent,* between the years 1920 and 1922.

———, in collaboration with Samuel Crowther, *My Life and Work.* New York: Garden City Publishing, 1922. Ford's accomplishments and philosophy of life, written during his late fifties.

———, interviewed by Fay Leone Faurote, *My Philosophy of Industry.* New York: Coward-McCann, 1929. Four monologues from Ford, facilitated by the interviewer, on the topics of machinery, industry, success, and progress.

———, in collaboration with Samuel Crowther, *Today and Tomorrow.* New York: Garden City Publishing, 1926. Ford's assessment of his importance and the importance of his company for the future of America, written just after he turned sixty.

Garet Garrett, *The Wild Wheel.* New York: Pantheon Books, 1952. Garrett attempts to show how Henry Ford's life and work played out before the time of government regulations in industry and economics.

William Greenleaf, *From These Beginnings: The Early Philanthropies of Henry and Edsel Ford, 1911–1936.* Detroit, MI: Wayne State University Press, 1964. A good source of information on Clara Ford, Henry Ford's wife, and on his son, Edsel, especially in relation to their public service.

Walter Hayes, *Henry: A Life of Henry Ford II.* New York: Grove Weidenfeld, 1990. A readable and insightful work on the grandson of Henry Ford.

Booten Herndon, *Ford: An Unconventional Biography of the Men and Their Times.* New York: Weybright and Talley, 1969. While concentrating on the younger Ford men, Herndon provides many insights into Henry Ford's life and achievements.

George H. Holmes, *The Reminiscences of Mr. George H. Holmes.* Dearborn, MI: Ford Motor Company Archives Oral History Section, 1954. A neighbor of the Fords in Dearborn offers his recollections of the Ford family.

Timothy Jacobs, *Lemons: The World's Worst Cars.* New York: Smithmark, 1991. Photos enhance this far-ranging account of the features that made certain car models unsuccessful.

Anne Jardim, *The First Henry Ford: A Study in Personality and Business Leadership.* Cambridge, MA: MIT Press, 1970. Attempts to explain Henry Ford's success through a study of his obsessions.

Robert Lacey, *Ford: The Men and the Machine.* Boston: Little, Brown, 1986. Epic of the Ford family and the Ford Motor Company, including their personalities, private tragedies, and public achievements.

Rose Wilder Lane, *Henry Ford's Own Story.* New York: Ellis O. Jones, 1917.

Carl D. LaRue, *The Reminiscences of Mr. Carl D. LaRue.* Dearborn, MI: Ford Motor Company Archives Oral History Section, 1955. LaRue tells of his experiences researching rubber tree culture in the Brazilian rain forest.

Samuel S. Marquis, *Henry Ford: An Interpretation.* Boston: Little, Brown, 1923. Personal essays by Ford's pastor and employee on topics ranging from Ford's attitude toward charity to his abrupt firing of valuable executives.

Charles Merz, *And Then Came Ford.* New York: Doubleday, Doran, 1929. Detailed, readable account of Ford's life and company, ending with the unveiling of the new Model A.

Allan Nevins, *Ford: The Times, the Man, the Company.* New York: Charles Scribner's Sons, 1954. Primarily a history of the Ford Motor Company, with a parallel focus on Henry Ford's life.

Allan Nevins and Frank Ernest Hill, *Ford: Decline and Rebirth, 1933–1962.* New York: Charles Scribner's Sons, 1962. The history of the Ford Motor Company after the company was no longer a revolutionary leader but was still trying to hold a position of surpremacy in the auto industry.

————, *Ford: Expansion and Challenge, 1915–1933.* New York: Charles Scribner's Sons, 1957. Covers the second period of the Ford Motor Company and details the sociological interests of Henry Ford.

James D. Newton, *Uncommon Friends.* New York: Harcourt Brace Jovanovich, 1987. Newton, who lived next door to Thomas Edison, provides an informal, neighborly view of Edison, Henry Ford, and others.

David E. Nye, *Henry Ford: "Ignorant Idealist."* Port Washington, NY: National University Publications, 1979. A study of Ford that attempts to reveal his symbolic meanings for the culture that grew out of the universal use of the automobile.

William Adams Simonds, *Henry Ford: His Life, His Work, His Genius.* Los Angeles: Floyd Clymer, 1946. Well-researched biography that emphasizes Ford's wartime production.

Upton Sinclair, *The Flivver King.* Detroit, MI: United Automobile Workers of America, 1937. Throughout this short book, written to support unions' struggle to organize workers at the Ford Motor Company, Sinclair contrasts the life of the Fords with the life of a typical worker family.

Keith Sward, *The Legend of Henry Ford.* New York: Rinehart, 1948. Favorable biography of Henry Ford that details many personalities.

Hans Tanner, *The Racing Fords.* New York: Meredith Press, 1968. A detailed account of the way in which Ford and the Ford Motor Company used racing to establish their excellence in car manufacturing.

John Wagner, *The Reminiscences of Mr. John Wagner.* Dearborn, MI: Ford Motor Company Archives Oral History Section, 1955. Mr. Wagner tells about his work with Henry Ford in the maintenance department of the company.

E.F. Wait, *The Reminiscences of Mr. E.F. Wait.* Dearborn, MI: Ford Motor Company Archives Oral History Section, 1954. Mr. Wait discusses his involvement with glassmaking at the Ford Motor Company plant.

Michael Williams, *Ford and Fordson Tractors.* Dorset, England: Blandford Press, 1985. Assessment of the tractor's impact on agriculture, with many photographs.

Periodicals

Associated Press, "New CEO at Ford Is a Ford," *Daily Inter Lake,* October 31, 2001.

Automotive News, "Henry Ford II Now President of Company," September 28, 2000.

Elizabeth Breuer, "Henry Ford and the Believer," *Ladies Home Journal,* September 1923.

Mary A. Dempsey, "Henry Ford's Amazonian Suburbia," *Américas,* March/April 1996.

Malcolm S. Forbes, "Two Giant U.S. Business Efforts that Failed in Brazil," *Forbes,* October 19, 1987.

Lee Iacocca, "Driving Force: Henry Ford," *Time,* December 7, 1998.

Peter Ling, "Henry Ford's Greenfield Village," *History Today,* January 1996.

Literary Digest, "Henry Ford Launches Another Novelty on His Country," February 1, 1919.

———, "Henry Ford Wants Cowless Milk and Crowdless Cities," February 26, 1921.

———, "The Latest Ford 'Joke,'" May 6, 1916.

———, "The Rise of Henry Ford," February 24, 1917.

———, "Young Henry Ford, Inventor," March 4, 1916.

New Republic, "Ford and Ideas," October 21, 1923.

Arthur Pound, "The Ford Myth," *Atlantic,* January 1924.

Margaret Ford Ruddiman, "Memories of My Brother Henry Ford," *Michigan History,* September 1953.

Albert Shaw, "Nine Governors of the Middle West," *American Review of Reviews,* May 1923.

John Tribbett, "Mangled Truths: Unmasking the History of the Ku Klux Klan," *Pulse of the Twin Cities,* August 22, 2001.

Judson F. Welliver, "Henry Ford, Dreamer and Worker," *American Review of Reviews,* November 1923.

Oswald Garrison Willard, "Why Henry Should Not Be President," *Nation,* May 30, 1923.

Index

Picture Credits

About the Author

Rafael Tilton, PhD, a writer and researcher who lives in rural Montana, has authored several other biographies for young people. She also pursues hobbies including gardening and desktop publishing. Tilton's background as a teacher includes encounters with many youths who, like Henry Ford, preferred mechanics to English and went on to lead successful lives.